Even More is an authentic and practical guide to help us discover our hearts desire. It is full of Truth-filled guidance that helps us get where we want to be as women—in a satisfied, content, and thriving place! The place where we see ourselves and He sees us and where we know Him deeper every day! I am so thankful for Rachel and Jennifer and their hearts for women knowing the Lord in a real and precious way! I highly recommend that you take this 40 day journey—you won't be the same and you will be glad of it."

KRISTI MALZAHN Speaker, Mom of girls, and wife of Auburn football head coach, Gus Malzahn

As a pastor in the trenches, I see the need for the empowering theology inside this book for so many. As a father of a teenage daughter, that need amplifies even more. This book will be a go-to resource in my home for sure. Rachel Lovingood and Jennifer Mills have gifted the church with a tool that will radically impact the lives of many."

DAVID NASSER Pastor/ Author, Sr. Vice President Liberty University

Journeying through *Even More* is like having 40 conversations with a godly, older sister. It has perfect themes for girls and young woman, strong biblical content, easy-to-understand application, and current examples written in the language of today's young women. This is a resource I want to share with my own daughter."

ANGELA COTTRELL Wife of worship leader, Travis Cottrell, and mom of a daughter

"Congratulations to Rachel and Jennifer for another GREAT book! Every father thinks of his daughter as a princess that is special. We fight against the pressure of the world to mold the thoughts of our daughters from the design God intended for them. Jennifer and Rachel give us a fresh perspective of a never-changing truth that God has a splendid plan for each of our daughters!"

SCOTT DAWSON Founder of Scott Dawson Evangelistic Association
www.ScottDawson.org

"I am very excited about *Even More*, the follow up to *Salvaging my Identity*, as authors Rachel Lovingood and Jennifer Mills continue to support a healthy notion of biblical womanhood. This is a much needed resource that will assist student pastors, small group leaders, and parents all over the country as they seek to teach the abundant life available in Christ Jesus."

BRENT CROWE, PH.D. Vice President, Student Leadership University

"In my years of ministry, I have rarely met a girl that has been totally satisfied with their life. We all have a desire for something more. The Lord wants to do more in our lives than we could ever imagine! Jennifer and Rachel do an amazing job of navigating you through a 40 day journey that will encourage and challenge you. Dive into this study and gain the knowledge of what it means for the Lord to do immeasurably more in your life."

LAUREN IVY Wife of Clint Ivy, Student Pastor at Prestonwood Baptist Church

"There are so many messages confronting girls and young women every day, but what they really need to hear is that they were meant for so much more! This book is a must read for any girl or young woman that wants to dive deeper to find out how to live an authentic life for Christ."

SHELLY JEFFCOAT Girls' Ministry Director, First Baptist Church of Naples, FL

EVEN MORE

RACHEL LOVINGOOD & JENNIFER MILLS

ISBN: 978-1-4300-4284-6
Item Number: 005754481
Dewey Decimal Classification Number: 248.83
Subject Heading: GIRLS \ FAITH \ SPIRITUAL LIFE

Printed in the United States of America

Student Ministry Publishing
LifeWay Church Resources
One LifeWay Plaza
Nashville, TN 37234-0144

TABLE OF CONTENTS

About the Authors 7

Letter from the Authors 9

How to Use 11

Proof 1 : Tastes and Desires 12
- Hungry?
- Who Am I?
- Words & Deeds
- Relationships
- Just Not Feelin' It?

Proof 2: Lifestyle 30
- Walk This Way
- Be All In
- Your Influence
- Exciting > Boring
- Be a Light

Proof 3: Confidence 48
- Why Are We Here?
- The Issue Is...
- The Solution Is...
- Unapologetic
- We Won't Be Shaken!

Proof 4: Fighting Tactics 66
- What Warfare Is Not...
- What Warfare Is...
- Suit Up!
- Defense vs. Offense
- Voices

Proof 5: Living Victoriously 88

- Start Small
- This Day
- It's Not about You
- Tangled Up
- Par-tay!

Proof 6: Freed Up 106

- Break Free
- Slave to Christ = Freedom
- Freedom & Responsibility
- Wise Thing?
- Freedom is Contagious

Proof 7: Stop Settling 124

- Go Deeper
- Step Out
- Push Yourself
- Watered Down = Not Attractive
- Choose Abundance

Proof 8: Audacious Expectations 144

- Nothing Is Impossible
- Miracles Still Happen
- You Don't Deserve It
- Dream Big!
- Gloriously Rich

Even More Wrap-Up 162

Discussion Guide 163

Journal Pages 174

Rachel Lovingood is a wife, mom, author, and speaker. She is married to Jeff, Senior Associate Pastor at First Baptist Church in Cleveland, TN. She has three children, two are married and one is in college. Over the past 27 years of marriage and ministry, Rachel has developed a passion to see people dive into God's Word and experience true life-change. She has written curriculum for years and recently started Impact Resources that offers strong, biblically-based resources for students and adults.

Jennifer Mills is wife to Brian Mills, and mom to McKenna and Parker. She is a speaker and the co-author of "Salvaging My Identity: A 40 day experience for girls & young women." Jennifer is currently serving at Englewood Baptist Church in Jackson, TN alongside her husband Brian, the Executive Ministries and Teaching Pastor. Jennifer is actively involved with girls and women's ministry. She has a passion for studying and teaching God's Word and seeing girls and women discover a zeal for the Word of God and for their Savior who loves and has redeemed them.

SPECIAL THANKS

We are so very grateful to our husbands for their unfailing support and encouragement. Our lives are *even more* rich because of the journeys we are on with you in ministry. We love you!!

Thanks to our families for loving us through the process of writing this book. Our prayer is that you never settle for less than *even more* of HIM!

To our LifeWay team—thanks!! Y'all have been a joy to work with and we appreciate the way you embraced our vision and helped us pursue it. Lives will be touched and changed because of your belief in this project.

...and to our greatest love—the Lord Jesus Christ. We thank You for Your Word and for the way that You have loved us and challenged us to strive for *even more,* all because of who You are.

From the Authors

Hey girl,

We are so, so, so excited that you've picked up *Even More*! This book is from our very souls and we are honored that you will be walking through this incredible journey with us over the next 40 days.

We're most passionate about this message. We believe God has given it to us to share with you. It's a message that can change your life. It's all about the life that He has called us to and we can't wait for you to discover it for yourself. It's so much more than we could have even imagined and that, my friend, is the key—letting go of what we know and think so that we can be open to His way and His plan.

Is your life turning out the way you expected? Is it better? Worse? Harder? The truth is that you can't predict what will happen, and your whole life could change within minutes. Maybe now it's a good time for you to stop being so focused on planning your life and instead begin preparing yourself to be who God wants you to be.

What if we become women who finally get it? What if we finally recognize that the abundant life is not about what we have or how we look, but it's about *even more*?

If that sounds even a little interesting to you, if you are intrigued by the notion of an abundant life, or if you are certain that there is more to life than what you're living now, then this book is for you.

Keep reading.

Commit to walking this path with us over the next few weeks and see what God has in store for you. You won't be disappointed.

We are praying that God will blow your mind and raise your expectations—because He can!

Sincerely,

Rachel & Jennifer

HOW TO USE

This 40 day experience is a journey through God's Word. Each week will focus on one of eight different "proofs" that give evidence of a life transformed by Jesus Christ. The proofs consist of five lessons that dig into specific topics. It is our prayer that these proofs will challenge and encourage you on your journey to fully embrace an *even more* life!

Change takes work and intentionality, so at the end of each day, there is a "Work it Out" section. This section is where you will find application questions, prayer prompts, and Scripture to help you dig deeper into the truth covered that day. There you will also find the "Proceed" section to help guide a discussion with an accountability partner.

At the end of the book, there is a "Discussion Guide" that gives you additional ideas for leading a group through each week of material.

We're always humbled and overwhelmed that God allows us to be a part of His transforming work by creating a resource to help girls raise the bar and go to the next level in their walks with Jesus. This piece is from our hearts, and we pray that it equips you to live an *even more* life that makes a huge difference in this world.

PROOF #1

TASTES AND DESIRES

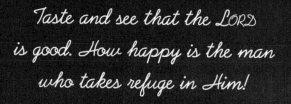

Taste and see that the LORD is good. How happy is the man who takes refuge in Him!

PSALM 34:8

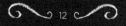

*D*o you remember a time when someone kept encouraging you to try some unusual kind of food, but you resisted because you didn't think you would like it (like sushi)? Then, you tried it, and WOW—it's now one of your favorite things! That can happen. But you've probably also tried a food, only to realize that it's even worse than you thought it would be. Unfortunately, that's been my experience more often than not.

Whether you are a picky eater like me, or you like just about everything, the truth is that our tastes—the things we crave—have a very powerful effect on our actions. Think about when you're seriously craving something in particular—like chocolate. Heaven help the person who gets in your way! How can a nice, easygoing girl turn into a crazy, get-out-of-my-way-now-or-else person? It's simple: cravings take over, and you lose control.

Cravings aren't just limited to food. We can crave attention, acceptance, love, and purpose, among other things. Like a strong craving for a certain food, our cravings for these things can feel all-consuming at times. That, my friends, is why we must look to Scripture and see what it teaches about these desires.

Taste and see that the Lord is good. How happy is the man who takes refuge in Him!

PSALM 34:8

Notice that Psalm 34 tells us to "taste and see." It does not say "taste and maybe you will see;" it simply says, "taste and SEE that the Lord is good." Unlike new foods, we don't have to worry about the Lord not living up to the hype. He will always fulfill and satisfy because that is who He is, and He can't go against His own character.

When you're walking with God, you'll will notice that your tastes change. You will begin to crave and feast on different things. You are motivated by different desires and tastes that will be evident in all areas of your life. Basically, you will turn from focusing on the things of the world to the things of God.

Over the next five days we will look at different "proofs" that you are becoming more like Christ. It's exciting to identify the ways that God is already working in your life and important to note the places where you can allow Him more access to change you. We'll cover a wide range of topics, from your relationships to your desires, words and deeds. We will focus on some ways you may have already been experiencing change as well as what to do if that change hasn't been happening. Get your taste buds ready because God NEVER disappoints.

...Now, time for a little sushi.

DAY 1

Hungry?

So rid yourselves of all malice, all deceit, hypocrisy, envy, and all slander. Like newborn infants, desire the pure spiritual milk, so that you may grow by it for your salvation, since you have tasted that the Lord is good. 1 Peter 2:1-3

Have you ever been around a hungry infant? Babies are unhappy and unsettled until they get their precious bellies full. And even though they're tiny, they're going to let the world know when they are hungry—and that they are unhappy about it! When we were babies, milk was all our little bodies could handle. It was the main source of nutrients for our growth, development, and overall well-being in the early years of life.

Wouldn't it be really strange if one of your friends whipped out a baby bottle full of milk at the lunch table? Definitely. Milk sustained us as infants, but we move on to heartier foods as we grow. Just as babies can handle more solid foods as they develop, we, too, can handle more spiritual truths as we grow as believers.

For optimal spiritual growth, we should seek to feed ourselves the best, most pure forms of spiritual nutrients. 1 Peter 2:1-3 points out that we *need* pure spiritual milk to grow. And with time, we learn to *desire* pure spiritual milk because we've tasted that the Lord is GOOD and know nothing else can satisfy.

As we "taste and see that the LORD is good" (Ps. 34:8), it should leave us hungry for MORE—more of the Lord in active relationship with Him through prayer, through His Word, and in corporate worship and Bible study with other believers.

You see, when we acquire a taste for God's goodness, we begin to crave things that are pure and holy. As our cravings change, so do our motives. As we dwell in the presence of God and experience His goodness, our goal will be to obey Him and glorify His name.

Jesus promised us in Matthew 5:6, "Those who hunger and thirst for righteousness are blessed, for they will be filled." Try not to focus on the word "blessed," in this passage, but rather focus on the phrase, "for they will be filled." The things we choose in our lives that please God will bring about fulfillment. Then, the blessings come when we're satisfied and full of Him.

When we're physically hungry, we become weak and lethargic until our bodies receive some form of nourishment. Similarly, we can become spiritually weak and lethargic when we're not communicating with God and spending time in His Word. In turn, this hinders our effectiveness in the work the Lord has given us.

Spiritual weakness makes us vulnerable to the lies of the Enemy. We begin to believe that other things in this world can fulfill and satisfy us. However, we were made to crave God—to know Him more, love Him more, and obediently follow His lead. God Himself put that longing and desire for Him inside us. Revelation 7:16 says, "They will no longer hunger; they will no longer thirst..." You see, girls, He's the only One who will fully satisfy. May we spend our lives in a constant quest for more of Him and what He has for us!

Let's start off this week with the following question:

What are the things that you desire, long for, and crave in your life?

PRACTICE (JOURNAL & PRAY)

❖ Spend a few minutes journaling about the things that distract you from having a genuine hunger for the Lord. Be honest with yourself, not focusing on appropriate "church answers," but instead on the truth. Then, jot down your answers to the following questions:

  ❖ *Do you crave spending time in God's Word? If not, why not?*

  ❖ *Do you desire to be around other believers who lift you up and encourage you to pursue Christ? Explain.*

  ❖ *Is your heart's desire to fulfill your own plans or to fulfill God's plans for your life? Explain. Why is it a better choice to live surrendered to His plans for you?*

  ❖ *Why don't the things of this world ever truly satisfy?*

❖ Confess to God the places and people you've looked to for fulfillment other than Him.

LINGER

❖ Reread: 1 Peter 2:1-3
❖ Dwell on: Psalm 34:8
❖ Memorize: Matthew 5:6

PROCEED

Use this section to keep moving forward as you apply the lesson to your daily life. Talk about it with someone you trust who can help you walk this spiritual journey with victory.

❖ Discuss your answers to the questions in the "Practice" section.
❖ Ask the Lord to help you crave Him above anything else—and He *will* help you. He wants you to turn your attention and affections to Him and ask.

Who Am I?

For the Lord sees not as man sees: man looks on the outward appearance, but the Lord looks on the heart. 1 Samuel 16:7b (ESV)

You've probably met people who initially seemed attractive for whatever reason, but your opinion about them changed after getting to know them. Upon seeing who they truly were, their "insides" weren't nearly as attractive as their outward, physical appearance. You probably learned at a young age that just because someone looks good on the outside doesn't mean his or her heart is beautiful. Still, we often judge people solely based on their looks, possessions, accomplishments, or social status. Think about the following questions:

What is the first thing you notice about a person when you meet them? Have you ever felt like you were only judged based on your appearance or accomplishments? Does anyone actually know the real you? Do you even know the real you?

There are definite dangers to placing too much focus on outward appearance. When we focus on attracting attention to a certain trait or accomplishment, we limit ourselves to being known by that alone. We're allowing people to identify us based on that characteristic instead of helping them focus on who we are—and more importantly—who God is. You see, God created us for a much greater purpose; to bring Him glory. Exalting His name through our entire beings should be the primary purpose of our lives.

As believers, we house the Holy Spirit in our bodies. (How cool is that?) First Corinthians 6:19-20 says, "Don't you know that your body is a sanctuary of the Holy Spirit who is in you, whom you have from God? You are not your own, for you were bought at a price. Therefore glorify God in your body." Our bodies were given to us for a much greater purpose then to simply attract attention for ourselves. But we often forget that truth. We use our bodies to gain the attention of others, which is such an empty feeling in the long run.

I remember shopping for jeans with a teenage friend one time. She was trying on pair after pair... you know the drill. With every pair she tried on, they got tighter and more revealing. She finally asked my opinion about her favorite pair. They happened to be a little too much of everything—too tight, too emphasizing, too revealing. I responded to her by saying, "Those are perfect if you want people to like you for the body parts those jeans emphasize."

We are being fed the lie that we will only find value and satisfaction if we look a certain way or have important accomplishments. But drawing attention to ourselves based on our outward appearance will never bring us the satisfaction we desire. And guess what? Our desire for attention shows that we are craving the approval of people over the things of God. We can so easily become consumed with promoting ourselves that we completely lose sight of seeking the Lord and finding fulfillment in Him.

As you seek the Lord, you will begin to care more about how you look to God and how you can use the body He's given you to glorify Him. You will begin to understand that when people notice you for what's inside, then God gets that glory because He is the One who makes anything good in us.

Look at what 1 Samuel 16:7 says is important to God—the condition of our hearts. Hair, makeup, flawless skin, and a perfect body have no eternal significance. God is concerned with what's on the inside. And we should be, too.

PRACTICE (JOURNAL & PRAY)

- In your journal, write down the first things you judge someone on. Then, answer the following question: How would it make you feel to be judged based on anything other than who you are?
- What evidence do you see in your life that you spend more time trying to attract attention to your appearance instead of your character?
- How does it make you feel to know that God cares more about your heart then your outward appearance? What do you think constitutes a beautiful heart?
- Write out a confession of any misplaced cravings you've discovered. Pray for eyes to see as God sees and for wisdom to be more focused on who you are over how you look.

LINGER

- Reread: 1 Samuel 16:7
- Dwell on: Psalm 34:10
- Memorize: 1 Corinthians 6:19-20

PROCEED

Use this section to keep moving forward as you apply the lesson to your daily life. Talk about it with someone you trust who can help you walk this spiritual journey with victory.

- According to Psalm 34:10, what will you experience when you seek the Lord, rather than the approval of others?
- Discuss specific things you can do this week to intentionally focus on using your whole self to point others to God and His glory.
- Hold each other accountable to focus less attention on the outward appearance and more on the heart.

DAY 3

Words & Deeds

And whatever you do, in word or in deed, do everything in the name of the Lord Jesus, giving thanks to God the Father through Him. Colossians 3:17

As a child I constantly heard my parents say, "Your actions speak louder than words." Now that I am a parent myself, I often use that same statement with my children because it's so true. It means nothing to me if my kids say they've done something just to get me off their backs, but their actions can't back up those words.

It makes me think of my heavenly Father and how He must view me as His child. I am someone who often says one thing and does another. *Actions do speak louder than words,* I imagine God saying as He looks at my life. It's not enough to offer lip service to God because He sees our hearts.

I don't know if you've figured this out yet or not, but our words also carry a lot of power. Luke 6:45 says, "A good man produces good out of the good storeroom of his heart. An evil man produces evil out of the evil storeroom, for his mouth speaks from the overflow of the heart." The mouth will speak what spills over from the heart.

I don't think we can talk about this topic enough, especially as young ladies—actually all women should be talking about the power of words. As females, we tend to talk... about everything. But all too

often talk can become toxic. However, when we pursue "even more" of what God has for us in our individual journeys with Him, our words —and the way we use them—will change.

We don't begin speaking a different language or pick up a new accent, but what we talk about, who we talk about, and how we talk will change. And the words we use shouldn't just change because we call ourselves "Christians" and follow an exhaustive list of do's and don'ts. Our words change because God has changed our hearts; we have been made new! What we once pursued as a means to satisfy is no longer enough. Our hearts are different. We are different. Therefore, our words become different as well.

Remember when we talked yesterday about the Holy Spirit dwelling in our bodies? God has given us His Holy Spirit to convict, lead, and train us in godliness. When we're focusing on pleasing Christ and allowing the Holy Spirit to lead us, we will no longer feel OK about talking about that girl on the soccer team, using bad language as a means to fit in with a certain crowd, or embellishing stories in order to appear more interesting. When we live an "even more" life, our words hold importance. As Colossians 3:17 says, "...whatever you do, in word or in deed, do everything in the name of the Lord Jesus." Our words should reflect Christ to others.

Our words aren't the only things that change as a result of Christ in us. When our hearts are surrendered to our Savior, our actions change as well. As we discussed earlier, our actions hold more validity than just our words. The proof of our spiritual maturity is seen in the way we live our lives. There's something that is different about us from the inside-out. Through our words and actions, we love and serve better.

We should always be striving to become more—more of who He desires for us to be both in word and deed.

WORK
IT
OUT

PRACTICE (JOURNAL & PRAY)

◆ In your journal, do a brief self-examination of your life. Do your words and deeds match up? If not, why not?

◆ Would your friends and peers say you have integrity? Why is integrity important in reflecting Christ to others?

◆ How are you using your words to point others to Christ? In what ways have you fallen short? Explain.

◆ How can you and your friends hold each other accountable concerning your words and actions?

◆ Spend some time with the Lord. Confess where you've fallen short, and ask Him to help you use your words and actions to glorify Him.

LINGER

◆ Reread: Colossians 3:17
◆ Dwell on: Luke 6:45 (MSG)
◆ Memorize: Luke 6:45

PROCEED

Use this section to keep moving forward as you apply the lesson to your daily life. Talk about it with someone you trust who can help you walk this spiritual journey with victory.

◆ Discuss areas in your life where you tend to say one thing and do another.

◆ Why are our actions so important if we are going to exhibit a faith that is more than just words?

DAY 4

Relationships

Whoever walks with the wise becomes wise, but the companion of fools will suffer harm. Proverbs 13:20 (ESV)

Have you ever had a pair of shoes that you just loved? They were your favorite go-to shoes for just about anything, and then one day they didn't fit any more? It's a heartbreaker when reality hits that those shoes that you LOVE just don't work any more. What could possibly happen to make you relegate something you had so enjoyed to the next bag of Goodwill® donations? It's usually as simple as the fact that your foot grew! That's a normal thing.

Although you will eventually stop growing physically, we should NEVER stop growing spiritually. This is exactly what we have been talking about in our quest to live in the "even more" mind-set of a fully devoted follower of Jesus Christ.

The past couple of days you've investigated some specific areas in which your tastes and desires are changing. Once your words, actions, tastes, and even desire for attention change, you will start to notice that some of the people you spend time with don't fit right any more. You'll seek different friends and a different community. In fact, an important part of continuously growing in your faith is

surrounding yourself with other believers who can help you grow, hold you accountable, and encourage you to continually follow God. In other words, you'll want to be around people who are also being changed by God.

That doesn't mean that you necessarily have to get rid of all your friends or break up with your boyfriend. But it does mean you shouldn't be surprised to notice some changes in your desire for certain types of relationships.

For instance, since your words have been changing, you may feel uncomfortable hanging with people who spend the majority of their conversations tearing people down, gossiping about others, or being negative all the time. This is a good thing! You also will be more uncomfortable with guys who are only interested in you because of your physical attributes and who could care less about your relationship with God. That's *very* good!

Scripture warns us about what happens when we aren't careful with the people we are in relationship with. Proverbs 13:20 says, "Whoever walks with the wise becomes wise, but the companion of fools will suffer harm" (ESV). As we crave more of God, we'll gravitate toward the people who reflect His character.

Be thankful that you are changing. It's a beautiful thing that happens as you grow more and more like Jesus. Notice what Proverbs says: "the companion of fools WILL suffer harm." It doesn't say that we *might* suffer harm; it assures us that when we surround ourselves with "fools"—those who aren't growing into the image of Christ—we will suffer at some point.

It's about way more than just trying to squeeze into shoes that are now too small. Your relationships directly affect your life, and the consequences can be HUGE! Choose to learn and grow with those who are also showing proofs of God's work in their lives.

PRACTICE (JOURNAL & PRAY)

- Take a few minutes to evaluate your main relationships and note where you've seen changes already. Where do you need to see more changes?
- Who are the five people you are closest to right now (excluding family)?
- Do these individuals point you to Christ? Explain.
- Pray that God will show you clearly how each of your relationships need to change. Ask for opportunities to share your stronger faith with those who you feel differently about because of your growing relationship with the Lord.

LINGER

- Reread: Proverbs 13:20
- Dwell: Psalm 1:1-2
- Memorize: Psalm 1:1

PROCEED

Use this section to keep moving forward as you apply the lesson to your daily life. Talk about it with someone you trust who can help you walk this spiritual journey with victory.

- Discuss Proverbs 13:20. What two approaches to relationships does this verse compare?
- What does it mean to delight "in the LORD's instruction"?
- Take some time to share any relationship changes that need to be made. Pray for each other to have the strength to follow God's leading in these situations.

DAY 5

Just not feelin' it?

If then you have been raised with Christ, seek the things that are above, where Christ is, seated at the right hand of God. Set your minds on things that are above, not on things that are on earth. For you have died, and your life is hidden with Christ in God. When Christ who is your life appears, then you also will appear with him in glory. Put to death therefore what is earthly in you: sexual immorality, impurity, passion, evil desire, and covetousness, which is idolatry. Colossians 3:1-5 (ESV)

Can we just be real? We know some of you may be reading through this first week and saying, *Hold up! This isn't for me. This is just too much.* We want you to know that it's OK. Rest assured that we're all works in progress. All we're asking is that you'll hang with us over these next 40 days. Push through. Seek what the Lord wants to do in your heart and life and watch Him show up!

We don't have a magical equation or three-step program that gives you the fire and passion to live for Christ. But we do have the knowledge that our God is good and true. He is alive, active, and in the business of transforming hearts and lives from the inside out. He just wants us to yield to His will and be open to His plans and purposes for our lives. To arrive at this place of surrender, we must stop seeking the things of this world to fill the void in our lives and look to Him instead.

If you're cravings in life haven't really changed since giving your heart and life to Jesus Christ, I challenge you to dive into today's passage of Scripture. Colossians 3:1-5 teaches us how to put to death our struggles in this life.

The first thing is to **seek**. Seek the things above, the forever things, the stuff that matters. Don't focus solely on the temporary. Seek after the things that glorify Christ and will last for all eternity.

Next, we need to **set**. Set our minds on things above, not on earthly things. We must get to the point where we believe wholeheartedly that Jesus is enough—where we focus on God, not on the things of this world or on Jesus plus something else. It's all about Jesus!

When we seek Him and set our minds on things above, He becomes our primary focus and the object of our affections. When this happens, our lives begin to look more like His. What we do, how we talk, where we go, who we hang out with, what we choose to partake in—it all changes. Second Corinthians 5:17 says, "Therefore, if anyone is in Christ, he is a new creation; old things have passed away, and look, new things have come." Our old selves have died to something better—JESUS in US!

In Colossians 3:5, we are challenged to put to death our earthly desires and replace them with virtues that reflect Christ's character. It's a choice we must make, but we can't do this in our own strength. We must seek the Lord to change our hearts and help us in this process. He promises us over and over again in His Word that when we seek Him, He will be found, and He will help us. When we are secure in Christ, our lives will reflect the very life of Christ in us.

So, here is a closing challenge for you today and for this week—pray! That's it. Ask God for to help you desire a deeper relationship with Him. If you're still fighting the desires of your flesh and this world, ask God to strengthen you and help you stand strong. Saturate your mind with His Word and surround yourself with other believers who hold you accountable. I guarantee when you've tasted and seen that the Lord is SO GOOD, you won't go back to your old self. You will have new tastes, and your cravings will be for the Lord.

PRACTICE (JOURNAL & PRAY)

- Close today by reading Philippians 4:8-9.
- List specific things you are struggling with as you work through this week's sessions.
- Be honest with the Lord. He sees your heart, and He knows what you're struggling with. Lay your burdens and struggles before God today, and let Him help create within you a hunger and craving for more of Him.

LINGER

- Reread: Colossians 3:1-5
- Dwell: Philippians 4:8-9; 2 Corinthians 5:17
- Memorize: Colossians 3:2

PROCEED

Use this section to keep moving forward as you apply the lesson to your daily life. Talk about it with someone you trust who can help you walk this spiritual journey with victory.

- Be honest with the Lord if you're in a season where you're "just not feelin' it" in your relationship with Him. Maybe you're craving the things of this world over the things of God. Share your struggles with a trusted mentor, accountability partner, or friend.
- Holding each other accountable when we struggle is such a healthy thing. When we begin to slide back into living out of "our flesh," we need people to pray with us and pull us back to the Word.
- List the names of two people you give permission to be totally honest with you about your spiritual walk.

PROOF #2

LIFESTYLE

Pay careful attention, then, to how you walk—not as unwise people but as wise—making the most of the time, because the days are evil. So don't be foolish, but understand what the Lord's will is. And don't get drunk with wine, which leads to reckless actions, but be filled by the Spirit.

EPHESIANS 5:15-18

*H*ave you ever bought a "knock-off" item? I once bought a knock-off Kate Spade© purse from a street vendor in Washington D.C. It looked so much like the real thing, and I just loved it—especially the price. But not too long after buying it, the purse started falling apart. The tag fell off then the lining ripped—and I hadn't even had it a month! I certainly learned my lesson about knock-offs: *you get what you pay for.*

Maybe you've never made the same mistake I did, but you've probably been disappointed in a purchase at some point in your life. Sometimes it happens because of our bad judgment; sometimes it happens because of false advertising. Either way, when a product doesn't live up to its label, there's a big problem.

We live in a culture that loves to label everything. From politics to brand names, from people to foods—you get the picture. Sadly, many people think it's cool to attach the label of "Christian" to their lives without actually surrendering to God and living for Him. But once you get to know these people, the label starts peeling off, and the lining rips easily. Suddenly, nothing about them resembles Jesus. Though they claim to be "Christians," that label has no effect on the way they live their lives.

"Christian" can be defined as "Christ follower." By claiming that label, your life should reflect Christ in every area and in every way. Your words, relationships, character, and lifestyle will be transformed because of Jesus' work in your life. If you claim to be a Christian but your life doesn't change, you're either guilty of false advertising or of being a knock-off. Being a Christian is not about simply attaching a label to your life; it is about conforming to the image of Christ through every facet of your life.

You may be thinking, "Why does my lifestyle matter as long as I claim to be a Christian?" Good question. Ephesians 5:15-18 points out the importance of one's lifestyle.

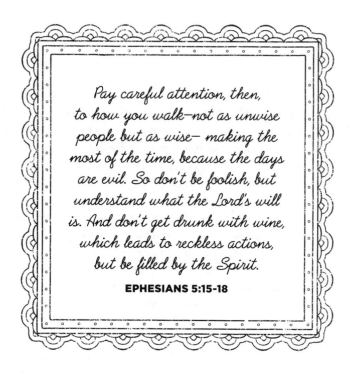

Pay careful attention, then, to how you walk—not as unwise people but as wise— making the most of the time, because the days are evil. So don't be foolish, but understand what the Lord's will is. And don't get drunk with wine, which leads to reckless actions, but be filled by the Spirit.

EPHESIANS 5:15-18

We're to live with wisdom and understand that, as believers, our actions point back to God. In order to walk like wise people, we need be filled with the Holy Spirit and follow God's will for our lives. These two things are doable and vitally important in living an "even more" type of life.

Over the next few days, we will dig into some different characteristics of a lifestyle that reflects Christ. Ask God to show you the areas in your life that need to be strengthened so that you can really live the life Ephesians 5:15-18 describes.

DAY 1

Walk This Way

I therefore, a prisoner for the Lord, urge you to walk in a manner worthy of the calling to which you have been called, with all humility and gentleness, with patience, bearing with one another in love, eager to maintain the unity of the Spirit in the bond of peace. Ephesians 4:1-3 (ESV)

If we're going to experience more of what Christ has in store for us, we must walk in a manner worthy of Him! Today's proof is titled "Walk This Way," but it definitely wasn't after the 1970s Aerosmith song. The title comes from the fact that we often need simple reminders to walk in the way that is clearly laid out for us in Scripture. In our walks with the Lord, it is inevitable that we will occasionally veer off the path. But even during the detours, I've seen God work in my life. In fact, those times often become journeys of exceptional spiritual growth as I corrected my course and aligned with the Father.

The Christian life can be such a beautiful journey, a journey of ups and downs in a fallen world. But the key is to simply keep walking. We must not give up, but instead stay consistently in step with the Father through it all. He is good. He is trustworthy. He is constant. He is faithful.

And so, we walk.

As Ephesians 4:1 says, we should "walk in a manner worthy of our calling." Paul wrote this while he was imprisoned for the gospel of Jesus Christ. He was ALL IN despite hardships, difficult circumstances, and opposition. He challenged us to live with the same passion and zeal that he had through it all. Our ultimate goal should be to live a consistent lifestyle, sold out for Jesus, no matter the cost. We should live "with all humility and gentleness, with patience, bearing with one another in love, eager to maintain the unity of the Spirit in the bond of peace" (Eph. 4:2-3, ESV). And as we are consistent in our walk with Christ, we will experience growth and change.

We can't stop walking. As long as there is breath in our lungs and we are given the gift of another day, we walk in faith. Some days it will be a thrill; other days we drag ourselves through dry seasons. But regardless of our circumstances, we must keep walking!

Consistency is huge in our walk with the Lord, as it can be one of the strongest proofs of our hope in Jesus. When we live completely dependent on Jesus, the world will take notice. Through the heartbreak and the joys of life, it will be evident to others that we possess humility, gentleness, patience, love, unity, and peace. We can't muster up these traits on our own. They are only consistent in our lives through Jesus being manifested in us. All He asks of us is that we obey and follow Him. Jeremiah 7:23 says, "... Obey Me, and then I will be your God, and you will be My people. You must follow every way I command you so that it may go well with you."

All throughout Scripture, we read about God's people who were stubborn and inclined to walk their own path. I don't know about you, but I think that sounds a lot like us today. We would greatly benefit by learning from their mistakes. Continue reading in Jeremiah 7:24: "Yet they didn't listen or pay attention but followed their own advice and according to their own stubborn, evil heart. They went backward and not forward." If we truly want to live this life abundantly through Jesus Christ, we must keep walking—not going backward, but always moving forward!

PRACTICE (JOURNAL & PRAY)

◆ Journal ways that you can "walk in a manner worthy of the calling to which you have been called." How can your walk influence those in your school, on your team, or in your family for Christ?

◆ Spend some time in prayer. Acknowledge that God is worthy, and confess the areas of your life that you haven't surrendered to His control. Thank Him for walking with you through every season of life. Ask God to give you the strength and courage to obediently follow His calling.

◆ Let the Holy Spirit examine your heart and see if you are bearing good fruit along your journey of walking with Christ. Growth will come as we continually walk with God. Where have you seen areas of growth in your life? What areas need more consistent work?

LINGER

◆ Reread: Ephesians 4:1-3
◆ Dwell: Jeremiah 7:22-26
◆ Memorize: Colossians 1:9-10

PROCEED

Use this section to keep moving forward as you apply the lesson to your daily life. Talk about it with someone you trust who can help you walk this spiritual journey with victory.

◆ Our prayer for you today is Colossians 1:9b-10: "... We are asking that you may be filled with the knowledge of His will in all wisdom and spiritual understanding, so that you may walk worthy of the Lord, fully pleasing to Him, bearing fruit in every good work and growing in the knowledge of God."

◆ Discuss some seasons—both good and bad—that you have walked through in your journey of faith. How has God brought you through? What spurred you on to keep walking?

◆ Discuss Colossians 1:10. How have you seen fruit and growth? How can you work on the areas of your life that need some tending to?

DAY 2

Be All In

"This is the most important," Jesus answered: Listen, Israel! The Lord our God, the Lord is One. Love the Lord your God with all your heart, with all your soul, with all your mind, and with all your strength. Mark 12:29-30

The tendency to compartmentalize our lives often keeps us from living like Christ.

What do I mean by that? Well, we tend to fall into a trap of thinking that we should be a certain way at school, another way with our family, and an even different way at church. In other words, compartmentalizing means that we break our lives into sections. Sadly, we sometimes believe that we can exclude God from certain sections, but that belief couldn't be more wrong.

When we give our lives to Christ and He becomes our Savior, He desires to change every single part of our lives. He doesn't just want to get us into heaven; He wants to transform our thoughts, our relationships, our desires—He wants to be Lord of our entire beings.

But sometimes we refuse to give up control of every part of our lives. We can buy into the false idea that it is more important to be "Christian" in some areas than others. WHAT? Does that even make sense? (It doesn't.) Think about your own life.

- *What areas of your life have you completely given to God?*
- *What areas are you still trying to control?*

Compare your life to a house with several different rooms. When you asked Jesus to save you, it was like inviting Him into the foyer. He willingly came in, and all was good. But as you continue to move about your house ("life"), there are certain rooms or closets that you keep shut off from Him. Sure, He can look at the foyer all He wants, but open up the closet? No, thank you.

Maybe you've surrendered your life to Christ but kept the door shut on your dating life because it is way too messy to let Him see it. Or maybe you refuse to let Him take control of your future, because you worry His plan may interfere with your dreams. There are a lot of reasons you may be shutting God out—worry, fear, a desire for control. But that is NOT being all in, and it isn't what a relationship with Jesus is supposed to be like.

Read Mark 12:29-30 again. It says, "... Listen, Israel! The Lord our God, the Lord is One. Love the Lord your God with all your heart, with all your soul, with all your mind, and with all your strength." Notice that it says we are to love the Lord with ALL—*all* of our heart, soul, mind, and strength. That means He wants to be in ALL of the rooms of your house and EVERY area of your life. He wants to transform us into the people that He wants us to be—people that love Him, serve Him, and glorify Him. We will never completely experience this total transformation while we're keeping the door shut on certain areas of our lives. As scary as it can be to let Him in to every part of your life, it is for your best.

When you refuse to give Jesus access to certain parts of your life, you are guilty of compartmentalizing. When you do this, you are the one who is missing out. He desires to do a work in your life, but if you refuse to let Him in completely, you will not get to experience that gift to the fullest extent. You must come to realize that there is nothing that you or anyone else can handle better than the Lord Jesus Christ can. Give Him control and watch Him transform even the messiest parts of your life. He is faithful to do it.

PRACTICE (JOURNAL & PRAY)

- Spend some time journaling through the following questions:
  - *What rooms/areas of your life are you holding back from God?*
  - *Why are you trying to control things yourself?*
  - *Why is it not wise to hold back areas of your life from God?*
- Confess your sin of withholding any part of your life from the guidance and control of the Lord. (Usually when we keep something back, it's so we can indulge our sin nature.) Thank God for forgiveness and for being concerned about every area of your life.

LINGER

- Reread: Mark 12:29-30
- Dwell: Romans 15:13
- Memorize: Mark 12:30

PROCEED

Use this section to keep moving forward as you apply the lesson to your daily life. Talk about it with someone you trust who can help you walk this spiritual journey with victory.

- Discuss the benefits you will experience when you surrender control of your life to Jesus.
- Read Romans 15:13, and discuss the following questions:
- *How do you become filled with the Holy Spirit?*
- *What will you overflow with when you are filled with the Holy Spirit?*
- *How can your witness for Christ be affected when you are fully surrendered to the Holy Spirit and are "overflowing with hope"?*
- Spend a few minutes praying for each other. Ask God to give you all the courage to fully surrender every part of your lives to Christ.

DAY 3
Your Influence

We do not boast beyond limit in the labors of others. But our hope is that as your faith increases, our area of influence among you may be greatly enlarged, so that we may preach the gospel in lands beyond you, without boasting of work already done in another's area of influence. 2 Corinthians 10:15-16 (ESV)

Do you believe that every person has an influence on someone else? You should...

There will always be someone who looks up to you, or is younger or less experienced. These people are in your sphere of influence. In other words, these are the people you encounter and influence on a regular basis. The definition of *influence* is "the capacity to have an effect on the character, development, or behavior of someone or something."[1] Did you catch that? Influence is simply the capacity to have an effect on someone. And your capacity to have an effect on someone is huge. Just think through all the people you encounter in one day. You can have a positive effect on all of those people!

While we can be positive influences, we can also influence in a negative way—and we must decide daily what kind of impact we will have. Sometimes, it seems inconvenient or challenging to positively influence those around us. But we're challenged by Jesus' brother James to not show favoritism (Jas. 2:1). Simply put, we are to live and love as Jesus did, loving and influencing all people, regardless of our levels of comfort. The evidence of what Christ has done in our lives should pour out of us, affecting and inspiring *everyone* that we encounter.

As Christians, we are called to love and lead well, regardless of our personality type or the size of our sphere of influence. We all have the ability to influence, and God will use us to further His kingdom and show His love during our brief time on this earth.

If you're thinking that you don't have very much influence, think again. For example, most of you likely participate in some form of social media, which is a huge realm of influence in modern-day culture. Regardless of how many friends or followers you have on social media, you have a captive audience. Social media and the Internet give us a natural platform to exalt the name of Jesus Christ. So, considering that influence, here are a few questions for you:

> ❖ *What messages are you sending out through your social media? How are you affecting the world around you? What kind of "footprint" are you leaving on this earth by your online presence?*

Begin thinking through these questions as you continue to post on social media. Remember, we can be consistent followers of Jesus through our lives, our love for God, and the way we empower and encourage those around us. There's no such thing as a small sphere of influence because we all have an impact on at least one other person—and that has the potential to change the world. Girls, that's influence!

We pray you're challenged to examine your sphere of influence. As you grow in your faith, you should be growing in your influence, and your influence should shape those around you. All throughout Scripture we see that people are a big deal to God. Therefore, they should be a big deal to us.

May we be women who inspire and build up the confidence of those we encounter on a daily basis. Let's be engaging and relevant to the culture as a means of influencing this generation. Let's have an effect on the lives of those around us for eternity!

PRACTICE (JOURNAL & PRAY)

◆ Influence is going to look different for each person. Spend some time in prayer today, asking God to reveal the areas in your life where you need to leverage your influence for Him.

◆ In your journal, write down the names of a few people you see on a daily basis. Consider the people you see at school, play with on sports teams, and sit next to in class. How can you show them that your faith is the real deal? How will you show them how Christ has transformed your life? What steps will you take to show them God's love?

◆ Review the questions about social media on the previous page. Spend a few minutes journaling your responses to those questions.

◆ Go to the Lord in prayer, asking Him to help you rise to the occasion and make a difference in this world. Pray for the courage to influence those around you in a positive way, pointing them to the only One who can make a real difference in their life—Jesus!

LINGER

◆ Reread: 2 Corinthians 10:15-16
◆ Dwell: Jeremiah 15:19
◆ Memorize: James 2:1

PROCEED

Use this section to keep moving forward as you apply the lesson to your daily life. Talk about it with someone you trust who can help you walk this spiritual journey with victory.

◆ Revisit some of the questions from the "Practice" section with a trustworthy friend.

◆ Discuss the definition of influence and what it means in your life. Examine your life and the areas of influence the Lord has entrusted to you.

◆ Speak edifying words into each others' lives about the influence you see in your friend. Discuss the impact you could make if you both leveraged your influences for Christ.

Exciting > Boring

The old way, with laws etched in stone, led to death, though it began with such glory that the people of Israel could not bear to look at Moses' face. For his face shone with the glory of God, even though the brightness was already fading away. Shouldn't we expect far greater glory under the new way, now that the Holy Spirit is giving life? If the old way, which brings condemnation, was glorious, how much more glorious is the new way, which makes us right with God! In fact, that first glory was not glorious at all compared with the overwhelming glory of the new way. So if the old way, which has been replaced, was glorious, how much more glorious is the new, which remains forever! Since this new way gives us such confidence, we can be very bold. 2 Corinthians 3:7-12 (NLT)

No matter what level of math you have conquered at this point, you are probably familiar with this symbol: >

This is the "greater than" symbol. It's used to compare two things and stress the superiority of one over another. You've probably even used it in a text before, because everybody needs to know that snow days > school days, or exciting > boring, right?

Today's Scripture passage is also a comparison that applies to some cool changes we can see in our lifestyles as we grow in our faith. Read 2 Corinthians 3:7-12 again slowly, underlining the things that Paul was comparing.

Did you get that? It's a comparison of the old way (laws and rules) and the new way (grace). We couldn't save ourselves from our sins in the old way. We are just too sinful. Thankfully, we have been offered a new way through Jesus Christ. John 3:16 says, "For God loved the world in this way: He gave His One and Only Son, so that everyone who believes in Him will not perish but have eternal life." Because of Jesus' life, death, and resurrection, we can be declared righteous before God. We only have to choose to follow Him. It's that simple! The new way is so much greater for us. We don't have to try to follow laws, we simply have to follow Jesus.

Paul, the author of 2 Corinthians compared "glorious" and "much more glorious." In this passage, he referred back to how Moses looked after he had spent time in God's presence. Moses was so changed from being in God's presence that he had to wear a veil to cover his face because the people could not bear to look at the glory of God that made his face glow. That's pretty cool!

What would it be like to look so radiant from God's presence in your life that it affected those you encounter on a daily basis? Well, if you read along in the verses, you see that Paul was saying that the glory Moses experienced was nothing compared to the overwhelming glory of the new way that we have the privilege to live in. Jesus' death on the cross and resurrection changed everything, and it gives us a choice to settle for "less than" or go for "greater than."

The cool thing about choosing to go for the greater glory is that it comes with an awesome result. Look at the last line of verse 12. When we choose the new way, the greater glory, then we will have more confidence and we can be "very bold"—and that is super exciting.

It makes no sense that anyone would choose boring over exciting. When you live a boring spiritual life, you only have yourself to blame. Everything about our God is exciting, and He is more than capable of blowing your mind if you let Him. The changes just keep coming and your life becomes more and more... and even more.

PRACTICE (JOURNAL & PRAY)

◆ Spend a few minutes journaling your answers to the following questions:

   ◆ *Would you consider your spiritual life to be boring or exciting? Explain.*
   ◆ *Why do you settle for less than exciting?*
   ◆ *What does it mean to you that God gave us a "new way"? Do you think you could get by in the "old way"? Explain your answer.*

◆ It's time to raise the level of your lifestyle. Spend some time in prayer, thanking God for giving us a "new way." Ask Him to remind you of His overwhelming glory and for boldness in your walk.

LINGER

◆ Reread: 2 Corinthians 3:7-12
◆ Dwell: John 3:16
◆ Memorize: 2 Corinthians 3:11-12

PROCEED

Use this section to keep moving forward as you apply the lesson to your daily life. Talk about it with someone you trust who can help you walk this spiritual journey with victory.

◆ What are some ways that your spiritual walk can be more exciting? When you refuse to settle for boring, what changes might you see in different areas of your life?

◆ How will truly understanding the glory of the "new way" given to us through Jesus give us boldness in our spiritual walks?

◆ Pray for each other to never settle for boring in your walk with God. Encourage each other to boldly follow where the Lord leads.

Be a Light

For once you were full of darkness, but now you have light from the Lord. So live as people of light! For this light within you produces only what is good and right and true.
Ephesians 5:8-9 (NLT)

Think back to the days when you were a little girl—those days when you may or may not have been scared of the dark. Remember when you'd see the shadows on your wall and think they were monsters? Yet when the light was turned on, it exposed the truth that there was nothing to be afraid of. We can rest assured that light will always penetrate through the darkness.

Ephesians 5:8-9 says that we were once in darkness. But in Christ, we're illuminated by Him who is the Light, and we're to live as children of the light. We are to take that light and penetrate the darkness of this world.

In the New Testament you will find the word *light* around 90 times depending on the translation. Matthew 5:14 describes Jesus as being "the Light of the world," and Matthew 5:16 tells us to let our light shine before men so that they can see our good deeds and praise God. Notice the word *shine* in verse 16. Jesus' desire for His followers is that we would illuminate with His presence and glory in our lives. Our "shine" will showcase His glory so that others can see Him.

However, if we're honest, most Christians today aren't shining in this world. Instead, we're living dull lives, void of any light. Many Christians look just like the world. One of the most powerful proofs of being saved, changed, and transformed by Jesus Christ is the illuminating glory of Him living in and through us. Because Jesus is in our lives, we should look different to those that we encounter, and that's OK. We were created to SHINE and people around us will take notice when we do. When we spend time with Him, we're illuminated by His presence through the beauty and glory from His Word. We become light-bearers for Jesus.

The people who live in "darkness" in this world dislike the light because it exposes the truth. But as believers, we don't have to worry about walking in the light because once we follow God, we have no need for the darkness anymore. That's not to say we won't struggle with our sins as believers—we will. But we no longer have to be ashamed because Jesus has already paid the price for our sins on the cross. Jesus said in John 8:12, "I am the light of the world. Anyone who follows Me will never walk in the darkness but will have the light of life."

We see in John 3:20, that "everyone who practices wicked things hates the light and avoids it, so that his deeds may not be exposed." This is where our role is so significant as light-bearers. We need to "turn the light on," so to speak, and penetrate the darkness, exposing the truth that there's no condemnation through Jesus Christ. Yes, the light does expose our sin and make known the things in secret, but don't forget that Jesus also forgives, extends grace, loves, and offers a life of great meaning and purpose for those who believe.

It's imperative for us to make sure our lives are a reflection of the Light and of all that He has done for us and in us! We're called to be in this world, amongst the people in it, but not partaking of it. We are to live with transparency so that others will see Christ in us.

We are by no means perfect—actually all of us are far from it—but we must live with gratitude, shining Jesus to this world from the inside out. We've been set free! We've been changed! We've been transformed into a new creation! May we therefore live as children of the light.

WORK IT OUT

PRACTICE (JOURNAL & PRAY)

- Spend a few minutes journaling your answers to the following questions:
    - *Are you spending the time you need with Jesus in His Word? Why or why not?*
    - *Are you allowing Him to shine in you so you can shine for Him? Explain.*
    - *How are you doing at being in the world, but not of the world? Explain.*
- Spend some time in prayer, asking God to remind you that you don't have to walk in darkness anymore. Ask God to use the light He has given you to show others His love and grace.

LINGER

- Reread: Ephesians 5:8-9
- Dwell: Matthew 5:14-16; John 3:20-21; 8:12
- Memorize: Romans 12:1-2

PROCEED

Use this section to keep moving forward as you apply the lesson to your daily life. Talk about it with someone you trust who can help you walk this spiritual journey with victory.

- Take a few minutes to revisit some of the questions from the "Practice" section with a trustworthy friend. Pray for each other that your lights will shine for God.
- Discuss the following question: *how can we be a light in this world together?*
- Hold each other accountable in how you live, what you talk about, and what you post online. Use your online presence for His glory to shine light in a dark world.

CONFIDENCE

Therefore, since we are receiving a kingdom that cannot be shaken, let us hold on to grace. By it, we may serve God acceptably, with reverence and awe, for our God is a consuming fire.

HEBREWS 12:28-29

*A*nother proof that Jesus is at work in your life is your confidence when defending your faith. This confidence will serve you well as you seek to influence the world around you.

Why is confidence so important? Well, as you grow in Christ, you will see opposition rise against you. When you stand for Christ, people will try to change your mind and influence you to stray from the faith. If you are confidently rooted in your faith, you will be able to stand against this opposition. Faith without confidence isn't very convincing.

Are you one who can stand against opposition, or do you crumble because you don't really know what you believe?

Have you ever tried to convince someone of something that you weren't too sure about yourself? It's not very effective. I mean, who's going to believe you if you don't even believe yourself? Compare that with listening to someone who passionately believes in what they are saying—those are the people who have the most influence.

Now, think about this: when someone tries to change your mind about something, how often are you influenced? The likelihood of you being influenced often depends on your confidence on that topic. A lot of times, people try to change your mind in small ways, like trying to sway you toward a different restaurant or outfit. But sometimes people try to change your mind in bigger, more serious ways. How do you respond when people try to change your mind about spiritual things? Again, your decision to stand strong or give in often goes back to your confidence level.

How confident are you in your faith? A lot of people who call themselves Christians have little to no confidence in their own beliefs. In turn, they believe just about anything that comes their way—whether it lines up with the Word of God or not. We must be aware of the opposition and influences that try to keep us from believing truth. These forces will always be around. And if we want to be confident enough to resist them, then we need to know God's Word and be confident in its complete truth.

Hebrews 12:28 says: "Therefore, since we are receiving a kingdom that cannot be shaken, let us hold on to grace. By it, we may serve God acceptably, with reverence and awe."

We have received "a kingdom that cannot be shaken," and we can live with a faith that is unshakable too. Now, here's the cool thing about knowing the Word and being confident in your beliefs: not only will your faith not be shaken, but you will also be a positive influence for Christ, bringing others to know Him, too.

Remember, people will challenge your faith. Christianity has always been under attack. As believers, we need to know how to defend our faith and stand firm on the TRUTH. The ability to articulate and defend your beliefs is called *apologetics*, and it's something we need to do on a regular basis.

This week you will have the chance to break down some of the basics of the faith so that you can reinforce your own beliefs. Building your confidence will help you stand firm when anyone tries to convince you that *all beliefs lead to heaven* or *it doesn't matter what you believe as long as you are sincere* or *as long as the good you do outweighs the bad, then you will go to heaven*. When you know the truth, you won't be swayed.

Take time to dig into these topics over the next few days and solidify them into your heart and life. Then, the next time someone brings up a counter belief, you will be confident enough to stand firm and maybe even be the one doing the influencing.

Why Are We Here?

So God created man in His own image; He created him in the image of God; He created them male and female. Genesis 1:27

We have the great privilege and honor of serving God Almighty with our lives. Our faith is the real deal, and we need to live like we believe it's worthy of our entire lives! We were created for so much more than what we sometimes settle for in this life. God created us for a greater purpose than just to accumulate stuff and go through the motions as we navigate through each season of our lives.

We are here for a purpose! People spend their whole lives trying to answer the questions: *Why am I here? What is my purpose on this ball of dirt we call earth?* Contrary to popular belief, this life is not about us or our happiness. But we're fed lies daily from our culture that tells us life is all about us, that we're meant to be happy at any cost, and that we should have it all. These messages can distract and confuse us from the truth of why we were created.

When you go back to the very beginning in Genesis 1, you can read about how God spoke creation into existence. God Almighty created the heavens, earth, and everything in it, and "it was good" (Gen. 1).

An intricate part of this creation plan was missing and it felt incomplete until Genesis 1:26-27, which says, "Then God said, 'Let Us make man in Our image, according to Our likeness. They will rule the fish of the sea, the birds of the sky, the livestock, all the earth, and the creatures that crawl on the earth.' So God created man in His own image; He created him in the image of God; He created them male and female."

God Almighty came with a plan to create humanity in His image and likeness. The phrase "His own image" in verse 27 comes from the Hebrew word *tselem*, which means, "a shadow or outline of a figure, likeness or resemblance to, not an exact replica, or 'a shadow of the original'."[2] We were created intentionally for our lives to be a shadow and a resemblance of God Almighty! How cool is that?

If He took the time to create us all in His image and likeness, then don't you think God alone has the right to answer our questions about our purpose? His will, purpose, and plan for this world doesn't hinge on us. We can't thwart His plans.

When we are walking with God, growing in love and knowledge of Him, and experiencing His presence in our lives, we will receive a great peace. And with that peace comes a gentle confidence when embracing His plan and purpose. Confidence is the "proof in the pudding" to a world that is searching for purpose and meaning. As girls and women who have a relationship with God, we can live by faith and with confidence, knowing that He has created us for a purpose.

This faith thing is the real deal, and don't ever forget it! Our God is the Almighty God, Creator of heaven and earth. He is supreme and sovereign, and He desires a personal relationship with each of us. And, girls, there will be great meaning and purpose to our lives when we are smack-dab in the center of where He wants us to be, doing just what He created us to do.

So, when we begin to hear lies from the Enemy or from culture and our confidence in God's plan begins to weaken, we must remember that it's more about Him than it is about us. When we're questioning what to make of this world, this life, and our purpose, we need to remember that we are simply created by God for relationship with Him and to bring His name glory. We are to live our lives completely surrendered to His will and purposes for us. We shouldn't try to over complicate it because it's very simple: this life is all about God. May we have the confidence to obediently do whatever it is that He has planned for us.

WORK IT OUT

PRACTICE (JOURNAL & PRAY)

- Think through the following question: *Have you ever been at a place in your spiritual walk when you've really questioned your purpose and His plans? Explain.*
- Take a moment today to journal and reflect on Genesis 1:26-27 and the fact that you were created by God in His very image and likeness. Let that leave an imprint on your heart and soul today!
- We must know this truth from God's Word in order to combat the lies from the Enemy and world about who we are and who He created us to be. Set aside time to get into God's Word and see the difference it makes in your life.
- Spend a few minutes in prayer, thanking God for His good plans for you and ask Him to help you to confidently obey His calling.

LINGER

- Reread: Genesis 1:27
- Dwell: Genesis 1:26-31
- Memorize: Jeremiah 29:11

PROCEED

Use this section to keep moving forward as you apply the lesson to your daily life. Talk about it with someone you trust who can help you walk this spiritual journey with victory.

- Discuss why it is important for us to know our purpose and live with confidence in the plan that God has for us.
- Take some time to share with each other ways that make it easier for you to trust and believe in God's plans. What other verses do you cling to for confidence in Him and His plan for you?
- Be intentional this week to pray for each other to remember truth when facing opposition and to influence others for Christ.

DAY 2
The Issue Is...

For all have sinned and fall short of the glory of God. Romans 3:23

For the wages of sin is death, but the gift of God is eternal life in Christ Jesus our Lord. Romans 6:23

Sometimes, I don't think I can take any more bad news. It can seem like terrible things are happening all around us. People are dying of cancer; kids are exploited and abused; women are sold into human trafficking. Evil seems to always win. When we see all the pain and evil in the world, it's hard not to wonder how things got so bad.

That's a good question. In fact, it's one that is foundational to our faith, and one people all around the world are asking. According to Scripture, there is a very clear answer to why things are so bad. Check out Romans 3:23: "For all have sinned and fall short of the glory of God."

Sin is the problem.

Let's go back to Genesis. After reading about where we came from and how we were created (Gen. 1-2), we come across the story of sin entering the perfect world that God had created (Gen. 3). Adam and Eve disobeyed God's command. As a result, sin entered the world (Gen. 3:6). From that day forward, sin has been an issue, and Romans 3:23 says that it's a struggle for us all.

Now, here's an interesting thing about sin: every sin has a consequence. Some sins carry more consequences than others, but

one is constant—death. Romans 6:23 says, "For the wages of sin is death, but the gift of God is eternal life in Christ Jesus our Lord."

The word "wages" refers to the cost of something, and the cost for our sin is death. Regardless of what our sin may be, we have all fallen short of God's standard and deserve death. You might be thinking, *But we all die eventually—even believers!* That is true. But the death mentioned in this passage goes beyond just physical death; it's talking about a spiritual death. Death in this sense is eternal separation from God.

That's why it's so important that Jesus died on the cross for us. He paid the price for our sins—past, present, and future. His death gave the gift of eternal life to those who choose to accept the forgiveness He freely offers. It really is that simple and powerful.

Interestingly, people who want to challenge or attack our faith often have explanations or excuses for the bad things that happen in the world. Some will say bad things happen because God is punishing us. In this argument, they place the blame on God, rather than themselves. Others argue that people who do bad things aren't really evil, they just express themselves differently. But we know those excuses are lies, and they are in direct conflict with the truth of Scripture. Anyone who buys into them is completely wrong. Here is the real reason why bad things happen: because we live in a broken, sinful world.

You and I need to know why bad things happen and who the real enemy is. Sin entered the world, and evil is the result. Our real Enemy is Satan—the one who tempts us to sin and spreads evil every chance he gets. He is the one who first introduced sin to Adam and Eve in the Garden (Gen. 3:1-5), and he is still offering it to believers today.

In a world that resists the concept of right and wrong, we need to stand firm in the knowledge of truth and know that sin is the problem with our world. We also must remember that we can choose to be a part of the problem or a part of the solution. The problem of sin will always be with us. But we know the solution: Jesus Christ. Proof that we are growing in Christ will come from our eagerness and urgency to share this solution with others.

PRACTICE (JOURNAL & PRAY)

- Take a few minutes to journal your answers to the following questions:
  - *Where did evil come from? Why do bad things happen?*
  - *Who are sinners? What is the consequence for sin?*
- Now, write down a simple explanation of how one can be saved from sin. Be sure to include Scripture passages, like Romans 3:23 and Romans 6:23. When you're done, we encourage you to memorize this paragraph so that you can confidently share the good news of salvation with others.
- As believers, it's sometimes easy to forget the seriousness of our sin because we know we have been saved and forgiven. But it's good for us to remember that without Christ, we'd be spiritually dead. Take a few minutes to acknowledge the ways this week that you've sinned against God. Repent of your sin and thank the Lord for forgiving you and cleansing you of that sin.

LINGER

- Reread: Romans 3:23
- Dwell: Genesis 3
- Memorize: Romans 6:23; 1 John 1:9

PROCEED

Use this section to keep moving forward as you apply the lesson to your daily life. Talk about it with someone you trust who can help you walk this spiritual journey with victory.

- Using the explanation paragraph that you wrote earlier, practice responding to people who ask you why bad things happen in the world.
- Pray for each other, that you would clearly understand how destructive sin is in our lives and in the world. Also, pray for each other to be confident in the only solution for our sin, Jesus Christ.

The Solution Is...

When we were utterly helpless, Christ came at just the right time and died for us sinners. Romans 5:6 (NLT)

Jesus said to him, "I am the way, and the truth, and the life; no one comes to the Father but through Me. John 14:6 (NASB)

Don't you love it when you're reading the Word of God and find stories about men and women who, though they lived a long time ago, are no different than the men and women today? We're a people who are prone to wander, and even people in the Bible could be a hot mess at times!

They tried to live their own way, making choices for themselves and going their own direction—just like us. We all sin. We're fallen, sinful, and unworthy, but no one is too far gone. The good news is that there's a solution to our sin problem and the mess we've created for ourselves in this fallen world: JESUS!

That's it. Jesus. He came to earth to be the solution, to pay the ultimate price for us, and to take the penalty for our sins. He came to restore a right relationship with us to the Father. In His love, Jesus died a criminal's death on the cross at Calvary to reconcile humanity to the Father. For some of you reading this, you've grown up in church and heard of Jesus' death on the cross since you were in the nursery. But as you read through this day, our prayer is that you truly process this amazing sacrifice and dwell on His love for you. Take a moment to be still before Him. Reflect on your life before you met Jesus Christ.

Jesus isn't just some figment of our imaginations, ladies. He wasn't just a good, moral man who taught helpful life lessons. Not at all. The Bible says in John 1:1-2, "In the beginning was the Word, and the Word was with God, and the Word was God. He was with God in the beginning." Jesus was with God at creation and after the fall in Genesis 3, when humanity's sin placed a barrier between us and God. So, Jesus willingly surrendered to the will of His Father, left His throne in heaven to come to earth, lived a sinless life, and gave His life for our ransom. In John 14:6, Jesus said, "I am the way, the truth, and the life. No one comes to the Father except through Me." Salvation can only be found in Him.

This is King Jesus. He is Holy, righteous, Lord, Savior, Friend, and Redeemer! He desires to have a relationship with His people and asks that we lay our lives down and surrender to His will and plan for our lives. He is more than a ticket to heaven or a life preserver for us to cling to when things gets shaky. He is the very Son of God, the Holy One, the Prince of Peace. He is Immanuel, God with us.

Read the following passage in Romans 5:6-11: "For while we were still helpless, at the appointed moment, Christ died for the ungodly. For rarely will someone die for a just person—though for a good person perhaps someone might even dare to die. But God proves His own love for us in that while we were still sinners, Christ died for us! Much more then, since we have now been declared righteous by His blood, we will be saved through Him from wrath. For if, while we were enemies, we were reconciled to God through the death of His Son, then how much more, having been reconciled, will we be saved by His life! And not only that, but we also rejoice in God through our Lord Jesus Christ. We have now received this reconciliation through Him."

This is the gospel, girls! This is the heart of God, and we have the opportunity to live for it. This means we can have CONFIDENCE in this life, not because of anything this world has to offer, but simply because of Jesus. He is enough! The key to our salvation is not Jesus plus something else, nor is it accomplished by good works. Romans 5:8 reminds us that "while we were still sinners, Christ died for us!" He saw the ugly, tainted, sinful, hot messes that we are and still loved us, choosing to endure the cross for us anyway.

If you have Jesus in your life today, live to honor Him because He loved you enough to die for you and also because He simply is worthy.

PRACTICE (JOURNAL & PRAY)

◆ Think back to the moment that Jesus stepped into your life. Spend a few minutes journaling about how your life has changed since that moment. If you don't know that you have ever asked Jesus into your life, you can do that right now by confessing your sin and need for Him. If you just asked Jesus to save you, tell someone. CONGRATULATIONS on making the best decision ever!

◆ Thank God for all He has done for you. Thank Him for loving you and sending His Son to save you from your sins.

◆ Evaluate your life right now. Are you sharing the solution to humanity's search for purpose and hope? If not, why not?

◆ Write John 14:6 on a note card and place it somewhere you will see it often—on your dashboard, in your locker, on your bathroom mirror, and so forth. Use this verse as a reminder that Jesus offers us hope through salvation. It's our duty, as believers, to share this hope with the world.

LINGER

◆ Reread: Romans 5:6-11
◆ Dwell: Romans 5:6
◆ Memorize: John 14:6

PROCEED

Use this section to keep moving forward as you apply the lesson to your daily life. Talk about it with someone you trust who can help you walk this spiritual journey with victory.

◆ Take this time today to share your story of when and how you encountered Jesus. Share about your life before Jesus and where you think would be without His grace, peace, and hope in your life today.

◆ Spend time in prayer, asking God to give you courage to share with others the hope you've found in Jesus.

DAY 4

Unapologetic

Then he said to me, "These words are faithful and true. And the Lord, the God of the spirits of the prophets, has sent His angel to show His slaves what must quickly take place." "Look, I am coming quickly! The one who keeps the prophetic words of this book is blessed." Revelation 22:6-7

All Scripture is inspired by God and is profitable for teaching, for rebuking, for correcting, for training in righteousness.
2 Timothy 3:16

Have you ever believed in something that turned out to be untrue? Complicated plots are the basis for popular TV shows and movies because they draw you in, and then surprise you with twists and turns to keep you watching until the conflict is resolved. While this may be interesting in the entertainment world, twist and turns in real life definitely don't make for confident atmospheres.

Consider this: you develop confidence when you know with absolute certainty that something is true. Our world tries to convince us that there is no absolute truth and that truth is situational at best. However, this is completely against what the Bible says. Such a stance leads to belief systems built on shaky foundations.

The good news for us as believers is that our faith is based on the Word of God, and it is UNCHANGING. No other book in history has ever been tested and challenged more than the Bible, yet, nothing in it has ever been found to be false. Scripture reinforces its own absolute

truth in several places like in Revelation 22:6-7: "Then he said to me, 'These words are faithful and true. And the Lord, the God of the spirits of the prophets, has sent His angel to show His slaves what must quickly take place.' 'Look, I am coming quickly! The one who keeps the prophetic words of this book is blessed.'"

The fact that Scripture is inerrant, or incapable of being wrong, is awe-inspiring and gives us confidence to stand firm. But that's not all—look at 2 Timothy 3:16: "All Scripture is inspired by God and is profitable for teaching, for rebuking, for correcting, for training in righteousness." The Bible is much more than just true; it is inspired by God and has so many benefits to your life. Hebrews 4:12 says, "For the word of God is alive and active. Sharper than any double-edged sword, it penetrates even to dividing soul and spirit, joints and marrow; it judges the thoughts and attitudes of the heart." We can be confident that the Bible is *always* applicable and practical for helping us know how to live.

It is amazing how many believers act apologetic about the truth of Scripture when asked about the Bible's stance on certain issues, or when they are questioned about their Christian lifestyle. People sometimes dance around the truth, not being honest about what God's Word says. Although we shouldn't try to offend people with truth, we also shouldn't be apologetic or timid about sharing it. We should share it openly and honestly with kindness and love. If we've really experienced the transformational power of God's Word, then we'll be happy to share it unashamedly with others.

Here's the deal. The lost world is not interested in wishy-washy faith. If you want those around you to experience the gospel, then you must be willing to talk about it with them. If you are too embarrassed or apologetic about the truth of Scripture, then they aren't going to be impressed with it.

After all, you have based your life on what God's Word says—why would you not be willing to stand on that truth when asked about it? When your life is proof of your relationship with Christ, it draws people to your faith and that's a BIG deal.

PRACTICE (JOURNAL & PRAY)

* In your journal, write down your answers to the following questions:
    * *When do you shrink back instead of sharing truth? Why do you think that is?*
    * *Why do you sometimes feel apologetic about your faith?*
    * *If someone rejects your faith, is it about you or Jesus? Explain.*
* Spend some time in prayer. Confess your lack of confidence to the Lord, and pray for more opportunities to stand on the Word in a way that makes a difference.

LINGER

* Reread: Revelation 22:6-7
* Dwell: Hebrews 4:12
* Memorize: 2 Timothy 3:16

PROCEED

Use this section to keep moving forward as you apply the lesson to your daily life. Talk about it with someone you trust who can help you walk this spiritual journey with victory.

* Discuss the following questions:
* *What does Hebrews 4:12 say about Scripture?*
* *What does it mean to you that the Word is living and active?*
* *How have you experienced God's Word to be alive?*
* *How should your life look different this week as you live out the truths of God's Word?*
* *Who do you know that might be more interested in the gospel if they heard some hard truths from Scripture and saw you being a person who is unapologetic about her faith?*
* Pray for each other to have the courage to stand on the truth of God's Word regardless of the audience or circumstance.

We Won't Be Shaken!

Therefore, since we are receiving a kingdom that cannot be shaken, let us be thankful, and so worship God acceptably with reverence and awe. Hebrews 12:28

My husband and I are currently in the process of building a new house. This is our second time to build and the beginning of the building process always seems to go by so slowly. I tend to get a little impatient with the process. These beginning stages, although not the most glamorous or exciting, are some of the most important steps in the construction process. Digging the footings and pouring the foundation are the first steps of the construction—and the most crucial.

Everything else is supported and dependent on this phase of the home-building process. A defect in the foundation of a home could negatively affect its longevity. The principle of a strong foundation can also be carried over into our spiritual walk. In Luke 6:46-49, Jesus talked about the importance of a secure foundation for our lives. As He said in Luke 6:49: "But the one who hears my words and does not put them into practice is like a man who built a house on the ground without a foundation. The moment the torrent struck that house, it collapsed and its destruction was complete." The foundation on which our faith is built makes or breaks us in the long run.

Building a faith of your own is crucial for you as an individual. It can't be your friend's faith or your parents' faith. Spiritually, you need a solid foundation if you are ever going to exhibit a confident faith. When the winds, rain, and fire come—and they will come, figuratively speaking, in your spiritual life—you've got to know beyond a shadow of a doubt that your foundation is firm and secure.

Hebrews 12:28 reminds us that we are receiving a kingdom that cannot be shaken. This is a great reminder that this world is not our home. We have the hope of a future kingdom that can't be shaken or destroyed. We can live by the promise in that verse.

The second part of Hebrews 12:28 says: "let us be thankful, and so worship God acceptably with reverence and awe." Because of all that He has done for us and who His Word says that He is, we can stand in awe! The God that we read about in the Word knows and loves each of us.

Being confidently rooted in a firm foundation will not only lead us to share Christ with others, but it will also help us stand firm as we face false doctrine. In our world, it is important that we can differentiate between truth and false teaching. There are many voices in our culture today that claim to have roots based on the Word of God, but are really based in other things. If you have never dug in and studied God's Word for yourself, how will you ever be able to identify the truth from a lie?

The Secret Service has a division of agents who work with and study our country's currency in a counterfeit department. Their only job is to study the U.S. dollar bills so that they will be able to quickly spot any falsification. They know every detail of the bills so they can easily spot counterfeits. They are successful because they've studied the real thing. Likewise, in our Christian faith we must study and know God's Word thoroughly to detect the false spiritual teachings that are out there.

If we don't know the truth of Scripture, then we open ourselves to deception by counterfeit truth. In 1 Timothy 4:16, Paul instructs us to watch our lives and doctrine. We are to watch out, holding firm to our belief in the truth of Scripture.

The foundation of our faith must be firm and strong, built on the truth of God's Word and resting on the Person and work of Jesus. However, it's not enough to just know God's Word; we also must be actively applying it to our lives. There's a beautiful confidence that comes from knowing and applying truth in our lives.

PRACTICE (JOURNAL & PRAY)

- Take some time to reflect on why you believe what you believe—not just because it's all you've known or it's how your parents have raised you. Dig into God's Word and ask Him to reveal Himself to you through His Word.
- Take a few minutes to journal about the following questions:
  - *Why do you think a secure foundation of your faith is necessary?*
  - *Do you think that your faith is grounded in a firm foundation? If not, how can you make sure that it is?*
- Be challenged today to get to know God more through His Word. Study the Bible, know it, and have confidence in its truth.

LINGER

- Reread: Hebrews 12:28
- Dwell: Psalm 62:2
- Memorize: 2 Timothy 2:19

PROCEED

Use this section to keep moving forward as you apply the lesson to your daily life. Talk about it with someone you trust who can help you walk this spiritual journey with victory.

- Discuss specific things you can do to strengthen your faith.
- Commit to reading books together to build your faith and leadership.
- If possible, look into attending a Christian leadership conference together. Growing yourself as leaders will make you more confident and secure in standing firm in your faith.
- Pray together that you both will find confidence in the truth of Scripture and discernment to detect any counterfeits in this world.

PROOF #4

FIGHTING TACTICS

Be serious! Be alert! Your adversary the Devil is prowling around like a roaring lion, looking for anyone he can devour. Resist him and be firm in the faith, knowing that the same sufferings are being experienced by your fellow believers throughout the world.

1 PETER 5:8-9

*A*re you familiar with the term "frenemy"? You know—someone who treats you like a friend in public but is not actually your friend at all. Sadly, "frenemies" are all too familiar these days. But the thought that someone could be both your friend and your enemy should be a total contradiction. No one should be able to coexist both as a friend and an enemy, right? In the long run, that person is actually not your friend at all and is really just against you. On a bigger level, we have a very real Enemy who pretends to be our friend, but actually only wants harm for us.

The Bible gives us lots of warnings about Satan. He tries to deceive us into believing that he is a friend, but he actually only comes to "steal and to kill and to destroy" (John 10:10). He has been referred to by a number of names, including the serpent, the Evil One, the Prince of Darkness, the Devil, and Satan. He is very much a part of our fallen world, and we need to be alert and aware of his presence.

1 Peter 5:8-9 says, "Be serious! Be alert! Your adversary the Devil is prowling around like a roaring lion, looking for anyone he can devour. Resist him and be firm in the faith, knowing that the same sufferings are being experienced by your fellow believers throughout the world." In this passage, Satan is compared to a roaring lion that is prowling around looking for people to devour. That's scary. I know *I* don't want to be his next tasty meal.

When you start living an abundant life of victory and power in Christ, your enemy, the Devil, starts looking for ways to mess you up and steer you off course. In 2 Corinthians 11:14 we are warned that the devil tries to disguise himself as "an angel of light." His plans are to defeat you in every area of your life. You are his enemy, and he has terrible plans to harm you. BUT God is greater than any scheme of Satan.

As believers, we have the Holy Spirit in us, directing, convicting, and leading us as we go through this life. We have God's very Spirit to help us in our times of weakness—those times when Satan is really trying to get you to slip up. Satan is no match for our God, but that doesn't mean that this life will be a walk in the park. This side of heaven, we will have to deal with an Enemy who desires for us to slip up and stray from God.

Thankfully, God has not left us to figure out "fighting tactics" against Satan on our own. According to 1 Peter 5:8-9, there are some things we can do to strengthen ourselves against the tactics of the Enemy. Note that we are warned to be serious and alert, to resist the devil and stand firm. That's a pretty good list of things to focus on, and the end result will be that the Devil goes away defeated and we are victorious!

This week we want to help you better understand spiritual warfare and raise your awareness of it. We are also going to dig into ways we can stand firm in the face of temptation and trial. You know, you aren't a helpless victim at all—you are a strong warrior for Christ, and you have been called to stand firm and resist the Enemy. You won't ever be able to do that in your own strength, but there is nothing you can't stand against when you walk in God's power.

As we learn about fighting tactics this week, let's strive to be the women God has called us to be, even when life is tough.

What Warfare is Not...

For I know that nothing good lives in me, that is, in my flesh. For the desire to do what is good is with me, but there is no ability to do it. For I do not do the good that I want to do, but I practice the evil that I do not want to do. Now if I do what I do not want, I am no longer the one doing it, but it is the sin that lives in me. Romans 7:18-20

After reading the introduction to this week, are you beginning to recognize the spiritual battle we live in as believers? We face a real battle every day with a real Enemy who wants nothing more than to take us out of the game. Girls, this shouldn't scare us or intimidate us because we know that "he who is in you is greater than he who is in the world," as 1 John 4:4 reminds us (ESV). However, there will be moments in your spiritual growth and journey when life is hard, and God seems a million miles away.

Sometimes, when things get hard, we try to find fault in someone or something else. I've heard people who are struggling say that they're experiencing a spiritual "attack" in their lives—and this might be true, but sometimes it is not. Today, let's look at what spiritual warfare is not.

The truth is that every believer has to battle their own flesh every day because of our natural tendencies to sin. We have to make a daily decision to surrender control to the Holy Spirit. Apart from relying on God's Spirit in our lives, we will fall into sin when faced with temptation because we're living in our own strength. Because let's be real today, NO ONE is perfect and we can't resist sin without the Lord's help.

We're all sinners, and we are only saved by God's beautiful grace. And sometimes people don't recognize that in their choice to sin there are consequences that may follow. These tough times are not necessarily spiritual attacks from the Enemy; they're simply consequences of sin in our lives.

Paul describes our struggle with sin in Romans 7:13-20. He said that when we sin, we know what we should do when it comes to temptation, but we don't do it. In fact, we often do the opposite. There are consequences to the bad choices that we make.

It's clear throughout Scripture that sin has consequences. One of the consequences is a break in our fellowship with God. Sin puts a barrier between us and Him. And because our sin is a roadblock in our relationship with our Heavenly Father, it must be addressed and confessed. 1 John 1:9 says, "If we confess our sins, He is faithful and righteous to forgive us our sins and to cleanse us from all unrighteousness." Our sin needs to be dealt with before God—we can't hide our sins from Him and nothing catches Him by surprise. Confession simply means to go before God and admit that you have sinned against Him. Amazingly, He is always faithful to forgive.

Though God is faithful to forgive, we often experience other consequences of our sins in our daily lives. For example, maybe you've experienced a broken relationship with a friend after she found out that you had been gossiping about her. Or perhaps your parents found out that you lied to them and they no longer trust you. Some consequences are very painful and cause distress in our lives, but we can't confuse these consequences with times of spiritual attack. Spiritual attacks are real and do cause difficulty, but painful consequences from sin are caused by our own hands, not the Enemy.

But be confident today, girls, that our God never changes, moves, or turns His back on us in disappointment. Our own shame and guilt in knowing that our sin breaks the heart of God may cause us to hide, but we can't ignore our sin. It must be dealt with in order to restore us to a right relationship with God. Even when owning up to our sin is scary or hard, we can take comfort in knowing that our Heavenly Father knows us and loves us. He already knows every time we mess up, and He knows the sin we're hiding from Him. Yet, He loves us and wants us to repent and return to Him. We can be confident that our Deliverer will help us triumph over our struggle with sin. In our flesh, we will struggle, but we can be confident in the One who has overcome.

We shouldn't call sin something that it isn't, but should deal with our sin head-on with the Father. Then, and only then, will we experience true freedom.

WORK
IT
OUT

PRACTICE (JOURNAL & PRAY)

◆ If you've been hiding or ignoring sin in your life for a while, take time to write a prayer of repentance to God, confessing how you've strayed and thanking Him for His forgiveness.

◆ In your journal, write out 1 John 1:9, and go back to that page at least once a day for the next week. Use this verse as a reminder of the importance of confessing your sin to God and making your relationship right with Him.

LINGER

◆ Reread: Romans 7:18
◆ Dwell: Romans 7:13-20
◆ Memorize: 1 John 1:9

PROCEED

Use this section to keep moving forward as you apply the lesson to your daily life. Talk about it with someone you trust who can help you walk this spiritual journey with victory.

◆ Discuss why you think we experience such a struggle between our flesh and our spirit.

◆ If there has been any sin in your life that has been causing a roadblock between you and the Lord, confess that struggle to your friend. Offer accountability to each other, and if the issue is too big to handle, find a trusted adult (small group leader, youth pastor, parent, etc.) to give you guidance. There should never be any shame in asking for help, prayer, and accountability.

DAY 2

What Warfare Is...

For our battle is not against flesh and blood, but against the rulers, against the authorities, against the world powers of this darkness, against the spiritual forces of evil in the heavens.
Ephesians 6:12

It's really hard to fight when you don't know who the enemy is. You aren't sure where the hits are coming from and what will be the most powerful defense against the attacks. That's why it's so important that we clearly understand spiritual warfare—we don't want to fight against everything and everyone. We have a real Enemy. He is not of flesh and blood, but is described as the force "of evil in the heavens." The Enemy we're fighting against is no joke.

The truth is that when you chose Jesus and became part of His team on this earth, you received all the amazing things that go along with being a daughter of the King. You share in His inheritance, you receive His Holy Spirit, but you also gain an Enemy. This isn't something to be taken lightly. Sadly, many believers are confused about spiritual warfare. We've already discussed what warfare is not, but now let's look at what it is. Let's decipher how to recognize a spiritual attack.

Satan loves to distract us from what God is doing. He is happy to offer us plenty of temptation to turn from God's plan and instead follow our own. And don't think you're off the hook if you are faithfully following the Lord. When we're doing the most for God and His kingdom is when Satan feels the most threatened. He will do anything to keep us from following God. Do you know what Satan's plan is for you? Remember what John 10:10 says: "A thief comes only to steal and to kill and to destroy..." That verse sums up the plans the Enemy has for you. He does not desire good for you; His desire is to steal, kill, and destroy. It's as simple as that.

So, how does he steal, kill, and destroy? The Bible doesn't contain a exhaustive list that explains all the ways that Satan works, but you can learn to recognize his practices and habits so that you are better able to stand firm against him. One of the names that Satan has been given is "Father of Liars," as you can see in John 8:44. Feeding us lies about ourselves and about God is one of Satan's favorite tools, and he uses it regularly. Those lies that you hear in your head when you look in the mirror or as you're driving down the road—that's him. The voice that says "You aren't good enough, pretty enough, or _____ enough"—that's him. When you find yourself believing that God can't forgive you or that you're too far gone—that's him. Those are all LIES, and they come from the "Father of Liars" himself. Our responsibility is to know the truth, because it is the best weapon against a lie.

The weapon of warfare Satan used against Eve in the garden was to create doubt (Gen. 3:1-4). Have you ever fallen prey to doubt? Doubt is typically used by the Enemy to stop us in our tracks and draw us away from Jesus and the life He desires for us. Doubt creeps in like an annoying whisper in your ear.

> *God won't really care if you do that.*
> *How can God ever forgive you for that?*

Although it is normal to question some of the things you read in Scripture, when we allow doubt to settle in, we are giving the Enemy too much power in our lives.

Another one of Satan's tactics is to make us think that sin is entertaining or fun. He influences us through culture—like when a couple on a TV show has flirted for a while and you celebrate them finally sleeping together, or when you cheer on the character with an alternative lifestyle because he or she is the most funny and endearing one on the show. That doesn't even cover the fact that we spend a lot of good money to watch movies where characters engage in behavior that is ungodly at best and often downright demonic. We call this our "entertainment." When we are entertained by sin, we become desensitized to it. Sin can be masked through entertainment, and this delights our Enemy.

There are plenty of other tactics that Satan uses, because he is a creative enemy with lots of resources. But here's the deal: Satan is a created being without the same powers as God. We don't need to fear him, because God is so much more powerful, but we do need to be aware that he is present and wants us to stumble. Though it may seem like it at time, Satan cannot read your mind. However, he does watch your behaviors and listen to you talk. Thus, he figures out your weaknesses.

One major thing to beware of is the way that the world embraces things of Satan and tempts you to try it "just for fun." Stay away from anything to do with Black Magic, Satanic worship, or witches. These things can seem popular in culture, but they are actually just invitations that welcome the Enemy into our lives. The movies and books that paint these practices as harmless are lying, and you should be very cautious of them.

We need to know what our Enemy is capable of and then do all that we can to minimize the effect he has on us. Remember, "the One who is in you is greater than the one who is in the world."

Our God is bigger and stronger!

PRACTICE (JOURNAL & PRAY)

◆ In your journal, write out your answers to the following questions:
  ◆ *What are some of the ways the enemy is creeping into your life?*
  ◆ *Where are you most unaware of his influence? (When answering this question, consider movies, books, TV shows, social media, etc.)*
  ◆ *What lies are you most vulnerable to believing right now?*
◆ Spend some time in prayer. Ask God to show you truth from His Word that you need to believe over the lies of the Enemy. Ask for wisdom to see where you are weakest and thank Him that He is bigger, stronger, and more powerful than Satan and his tactics.

LINGER

◆ Reread: Ephesians 6:12
◆ Dwell: John 8:44
◆ Memorize: 1 John 4:4

PROCEED

Use this section to keep moving forward as you apply the lesson to your daily life. Talk about it with someone you trust who can help you walk this spiritual journey with victory.

◆ Identify your areas of weakness and discuss them with your friend. Be specific about the situations, people, and so forth. Discuss why it is easier to believe the lies than the truth sometimes.
◆ Search for a few verses that speak truth to counteract the lies of the Enemy. Choose some to memorize together.
◆ Pray and encourage each other to be wise about the Enemy's tactics. When you feel an attack, speak the name of Jesus and follow His example of quoting Scripture.

DAY
3

Suit Up!

Therefore put on the full armor of God, so that when the day of evil comes, you may be able to stand your ground, and after you have done everything, to stand. Ephesians 6:13 (NIV)

We can all testify that just because someone has accepted Jesus Christ, it doesn't mean they're guaranteed ultimate comfort, wealth, and earthly blessings. In fact, sometimes it's quite the opposite. Our reality as believers in Jesus Christ is that we have a real, present Enemy in this world. There's a war waging against every Christian, as well as the church, and his goal is to hinder our growth and stall the success of the kingdom of God.

As Christians, we can find great peace and comfort in Jesus' words in John 16:33. He tells us to expect trouble and heartache in this world, but to be courageous because He has overcome the world! His power and authority is greater than anything we might face in this life. We can get excited because we know how the battle will ultimately end, but we still need to be equipped and prepared to endure it while we're living on this earth.

As we read Ephesians 6:13, it's interesting to note that Paul was writing this letter to the churches in Ephesus while he was in a Roman prison. He was chained for proclaiming the name of Jesus Christ. Paul knew what it meant to face opposition in this life because of the gospel. With passion and zeal, Paul wrote from his

77

place of imprisonment and challenged believers to "be strong in the Lord and in his mighty power" and to "put on the full armor of God, so that you can take your stand against the devil's schemes" (Eph. 6:10-11, NIV).

In Ephesians 6:12, Paul spells out who our battle is against—we talked about this yesterday. And in verse 13, leading into the actual description of the armor, he reminded us again to "put on the full armor of God, so that when the day of evil comes, you may be able to stand your ground, and after you have done everything, to stand."

Paul knew that we can only live in victory over Satan by relying on the power of Jesus Christ. Through Him alone we have the strength to stand confident and victorious in this battle. That's why it's so crucial for us to understand the importance of "suiting up" for the battle every day. Girls, we must be equipped and prepared! Our Enemy does not show us mercy or hold back. Satan does not wait for us to suit up in the full armor. He seizes every opportunity to attack, especially when we're vulnerable or don't expect it. That's simply the way he works. He's crafty and strategic in how he operates.

I know the majority of girls may not get into the whole metaphor of "a soldier preparing for a war," but whether we relate or not, this is our reality from a spiritual standpoint. We can pretend all day that passages like Ephesians 6; 1 Peter 5:8-9; and John 10:10 are merely fantasy or metaphorical. But, as all of the words in Scripture, they are completely, 100 percent true. We need to take the reality of this battle to heart and begin to engage in the fight that's going on all around us every day.

When we begin to see our lives and this world through the lens of Scripture, it changes us and shapes our perspective on everything. It's critical for us to take a stand, ladies. It's time to suit up and prepare to fight our real Enemy, because he's coming for us whether we're ready or not.

So, what armor do we need exactly? Ephesians 6:14-17 explains, "Stand, therefore, with truth like a belt around your waist, righteousness like armor on your chest, and your feet sandaled with readiness for the gospel of peace. In every situation take the shield of faith, and with it you will be able to extinguish all the flaming arrows of the evil one. Take the helmet of salvation, and the sword of the

Spirit, which is God's word." That may sound like a lot of armor to you, but would you go into an actual battle without any protection? No way! You'd suit up, because that's the key to survival. Spiritually, we must suit up as well. Going without our spiritual armor every day is like showing up to a war zone in a swimsuit. That's how vulnerable we are without the armor God has provided for us.

Not only do we need our armor when fighting the Enemy, we also need our weapon—God's Word. We must be women of the Word who are smart, strong, and mighty. As Ephesians 6 goes on to say, let's "pray at all times in the Spirit with every prayer and request, and stay alert in this with all perseverance and intercession for all the saints" (v. 18). May we be ready to take on the Enemy, fully equipped with the strength that God has given us to stand against Satan's schemes.

Are you ready?

WORK **IT** OUT

PRACTICE (JOURNAL & PRAY)

◆ In your journal, write your answers to the following questions:

◆ *How often do you think about the battle we face on a daily basis?*

◆ *How do you prepare for the day? Most of us run out the door all "dressed up" in our physical appearance but spiritually vulnerable. Consider a new plan of action using the prayer below.*

LINGER

◆ Reread: Ephesians 6:13
◆ Dwell: Ephesians 6:14-17
◆ Memorize: Ephesians 6:18

PROCEED

Use this section to keep moving forward as you apply the lesson to your daily life. Talk about it with someone you trust who can help you walk this spiritual journey with victory.

◆ Begin to pray the following prayer over your life every day.

"Dear Lord, as I get out of bed today, I know I'm stepping onto a battlefield. But I also know You've given me everything I need to stand firm. So, in the power of Your Holy Spirit, I put on the armor of God. First, I place the helmet of salvation on my head. Protect my mind and imagination. Guard my eyes, allowing no sin to creep in. Focus my thoughts on eternal things. Let the breastplate of righteousness keep my heart and emotions safe. I pray that I won't be governed by my feelings, but by truth. Wrap Your Word around me like a belt. Safeguard me from error. Plant my feet in Your truth and make me ready with the gospel of peace. Empower me to stand firm against attack. Give me the shield of faith. Protect me from Satan's fiery arrows. Place me shoulder-to-shoulder with Your army to oppose the Devil's schemes. Finally, I take up the sword of the Spirit, Your Word. Help me to read the Bible in a fresh, exciting way so I will always be ready to deflect attacks and pierce hearts with Your truth. I know I'll face assaults today, Lord. Give me strength for the battle ahead."

◆ Discuss how your days might be different if you took time to suit up. List the armor on your bathroom mirror or somewhere you will see every morning and pray it on as you get ready for your day.

Defense vs. Offense

Pray at all times in the Spirit with every prayer and request, and stay alert in this with all perseverance and intercession for all the saints. Pray also for me, that the message may be given to me when I open my mouth to make known with boldness the mystery of the gospel. For this I am an ambassador in chains. Pray that I might be bold enough in Him to speak as I should. Ephesians 6:18-20

One football season, our team was undefeated. We went 15-0 and eventually won the state championship. My son was on that team, and I would always get nervous about whether or not we could win each game. As the season progressed, the games got tougher and tougher. As we were driving to the stadium for game 13, I asked my hubby (who is very knowledgeable about football) if he thought we were going to win. He told me "If we score more than the other team, we will win." DUH, I knew that! But he went on to tell me that our team had a strong offense, and if we scored every time we had the ball, then there was a good chance that our weaker defense wouldn't be an issue. He was right.

We won and scored multiple times that night. And that's when it hit me—the best defense is a good offense! Guess what? That concept not only works in football, but it works in our spiritual lives as well. We have a real Enemy that is out to get us, and, sometimes, it feels like we are always on defense. We are constantly ducking the darts he is throwing our way or defending ourselves against temptations.

It's time for us to go on offense. We are on the winning team—when are we going to start living like it? We serve the God of the universe who is more powerful than anything or anyone who might come against us. We don't have to sit in fear or hide under the covers. We need to stand strong against the Enemy by living bold lives that push back darkness. After all, the best defense is a good offense, and our offense is stronger than any attack we could receive.

Yesterday you studied about the power of putting on the full armor of God to help you against the Enemy's attack. Today, let's look at other warfare tactics. Consider Ephesians 6:17-20: "Take the helmet of salvation, and the sword of the Spirit, which is God's word. Pray at all times in the Spirit with every prayer and request, and stay alert in this with all perseverance and intercession for all the saints. Pray also for me, that the message may be given to me when I open my mouth to make known with boldness the mystery of the gospel. For this I am an ambassador in chains. Pray that I might be bold enough in Him to speak as I should." What instructions do you find in this passage? We are told to pray at all times, stay alert, persevere, intercede, and pray for boldness.

Hmmm. The man who wrote these verses was one of the boldest people in all of Scripture. The apostle Paul lived a life of faith that showed no signs of fear, yet he asked that the people pray for him to have boldness. Maybe that was his secret. He didn't have the boldness he needed in his own strength, but he recognized that he had a supernatural boldness that only comes from the Holy Spirit.

Guess what? You and I are also called to boldness when facing the Enemy's attacks. We, too, are called to pray at all times, stay alert, persevere, intercede, and pray for boldness. Why? Well, there are a few reasons that our boldness against the Enemy is important. For one, we must be bold so we don't give in to temptation and disobey God. Two, we need boldness to stand strong because we don't want to be distracted from our mission—to go into all the world and make disciples (Matt. 28:19-20). In this crazy culture we live in and with the aggressive Enemy we face, it takes courage and boldness to stand, so we better start praying like Paul did.

WORK IT OUT

PRACTICE (JOURNAL & PRAY)

- In your journal, write down your answers to the following questions:
  - *How do you gain confidence in your faith?*
  - *What are the places/situations that cause you the most fear when you think about standing strong in your faith? Why?*
  - *How has fear kept you from being a bold witness that is actively pushing back darkness?*
  - *What would your life look like if you were more bold? Who would you talk to about Jesus? How would you stand firm against attacks from the enemy?*
- Spend a few minutes in prayer, asking God to give you boldness to stand against the Enemy. Thank Him for giving you His guidance and strength each and every day.

LINGER
- Reread: Ephesians 6:18-20
- Dwell: Ephesians 6:13-20
- Memorize: Mark 12:30

PROCEED
Use this section to keep moving forward as you apply the lesson to your daily life. Talk about it with someone you trust who can help you walk this spiritual journey with victory.

- Discuss how the words of Mark 12:30 can help you have a stronger offense in your home, at your school, at practice, etc.
- Spend some time talking through what your life would look like if you were more bold (from the "Practice" section). Encourage each other to live that life and pray for each other to have a supernatural boldness.

The one who enters by the door is the shepherd of the sheep. The doorkeeper opens it for him, and the sheep hear his voice. He calls his own sheep by name and leads them out. When he has brought all his own outside, he goes ahead of them. The sheep follow him because they recognize his voice. They will never follow a stranger; instead they will run away from him, because they don't recognize the voice of strangers. John 10:2-5

There is no denying that we live in a loud society with a lot of noise and clamor, begging for our attention. We hear numerous voices—some good, some bad, some questionable, and some, even from within the "church world," that can lead us astray. Today, we want to equip you with the Word to decipher truth amidst all the noise.

As we are wrapping up this week on our fighting tactics as believers, let's look at a parable from John 10 that illustrates our relationship to Jesus and how easily we, His "sheep," are led astray by other voices (vv. 2-5). In verse 3, Jesus said, "...the sheep hear His voice. He calls his own sheep by name and leads them out."

How many times in life do we pray to hear God's will or direction for our lives? A lot. We're constantly asking God to lead us, but, our Shepherd knows us by name. If we continue to grow and teach ourselves to hear His voice above all others, we can be confident that

He will show us where to go. The passage in John 10 goes on to say that He will go ahead of us and we follow because we recognize His voice. In verse 5, Jesus said, "They will never follow a stranger; instead they will run away from him, because they don't recognize the voice of strangers." We must be so familiar with His voice that we hear it above any other voice.

In verse 11 Jesus stated, "I am the good shepherd. The good shepherd lays down his life for the sheep." We have to know that He is good and has laid down His life for us. So, how do we know His voice? How do we make sure it stands out above all the rest?

First, we have to submit our lives and wills to the Shepherd. We must stop trying to do things our way or the way other "voices" tell us we should. Our focus should be on God alone. If you think about the job of a shepherd, it is both a noun and a verb. A shepherd is a person whose job is to tend to the sheep, but a shepherd also guides and guards the herd. Shepherds guard the sheep by looking out for dangerous predators that may be lurking around trying to get one of the sheep. Ladies, this is who Jesus is for us—the One who takes care of us, guides us, and protects us. Our first step is to submit to Him and allow Jesus to lead and guide us as a Shepherd who knows what's best for us.

Secondly, in order to recognize His voice above the rest, we must KNOW it. Sounds simple, right? We simply know Him and can hear His voice through spending time in His Word. We also must spend time in prayer, taking the time to listen and not just talk. If we do all the talking and don't listen to hear back from Him, how will we ever learn to recognize His voice? It's important that we take time to listen.

Sometimes, our prayers can be more of a monologue than a dialogue. We are often so concerned with rattling off our prayers of needs and desires that we miss the beauty that is found in sitting quietly before our Shepherd and actually waiting and listening for Him to speak to us.

Not only do we live in a loud society with a lot of voices, but we're also insanely busy, and we don't like to sit and wait for anything. A friend challenged me with this in my own prayer life just a few weeks ago. She said that if we will learn to linger and wait for Him to speak, He will then initiate, and we can respond. That's when intimacy with Jesus truly begins.

As godly women, if we can learn to linger in our prayer time with Jesus and carve out time to sit in what sometimes feels like "awkward silence," that's when we will hear the voice of our Shepherd speaking. We may not hear Him audibly—or at least I have never heard Him in that manner—but we will recognize His Spirit speaking. It's that still, small voice whispering to our souls and speaking life-giving words of truth, wisdom, guidance, love, and grace when we need it most!

In the life of every believer, we hear the voice of our Shepherd, but there are also times when we hear whispers from the great Deceiver, Satan. These lies and deceit can lead us astray if we're not careful. We must be careful not to open our hearts and minds to the lies that can drown out the truth.

We must learn to hear the voice of truth from our Good Shepherd that will always overcome any lies of darkness from the Devil. James 4:7 says, "Therefore, submit to God. But resist the Devil, and he will flee from you." Notice the two-part action steps in this passage: we must submit to God, and then resist the devil. We must cut off the lies in order to overcome and hear the truth. And we can't just hear, but we must submit to God by then following His leading.

When the noise of life becomes too overwhelming, pause. Open God's Word and listen for the voice of your Good Shepherd who has given His very life for you. He's tending to you and calling your name. You just need to learn to hear His voice above the rest.

Jesus said it this way: "My sheep hear My voice, I know them, and they follow Me. I give them eternal life, and they will never perish—ever! No one will snatch them out of My hand" (John 10:27-28).

PRACTICE (JOURNAL & PRAY)

* In your journal, write down your answers to the following questions:
    * *What are some of the voices that you've been listening to other than the voice from the Good Shepherd? Why do you listen to these voices?*
    * *What are some steps you need to take in order to hear and recognize God's voice better?*
* Take a few minutes to confess the times your heart has believed lies from the Enemy above the truth of God's Word. Thank Jesus for being your Good Shepherd, and ask Him to help you obediently follow His voice.

LINGER

* Reread: John 10:1-30
* Dwell: John 10:11
* Memorize: James 4:7

PROCEED

Use this section to keep moving forward as you apply the lesson to your daily life. Talk about it with someone you trust who can help you walk this spiritual journey with victory.

* Discuss some actions steps you can take to better know and discern God's voice.
* Read John 10:1-30 together. Break it apart and discuss the parallels between Jesus and a shepherd. Discuss what it means to have Jesus as our Good Shepherd.
* Make a list of some of the common lies you hear in culture, and find verses to counteract those lies with the truth of God's Word.

LIVING VICTORIOUSLY

Because whatever has been born of God conquers the world. This is the victory that has conquered the world: our faith. And who is the one who conquers the world but the one who believes that Jesus is the Son of God?

1 JOHN 5:4-5

How competitive are you? Are you obsessed with winning anything and everything that you're involved in? Recently there was a big uproar in the media about two high school girls basketball teams who were both disqualified while playing in the regional championship. They didn't cheat or do anything underhanded to achieve victory. Actually, the problem was that they both were trying to lose the game!

You may be thinking, *That makes no sense*, and it doesn't. Except that whoever won the game would have to then face the number one ranked team before advancing to the state tournament. Whoever lost would face a lesser skilled opponent, therefore having a better chance of advancing to the state tournament. Ultimately neither team had the opportunity to keep going, and they probably all learned a valuable lesson.

It wasn't making any sense to me. I thought, *How can anyone be sure that those teams were trying not to win?* So, I watched the video of different portions of the game and the commentators kept talking about how obvious it was that the players were trying to give the game away. And guess what? It *was* obvious. You could tell by watching them that they purposely did things to keep from winning. They purposefully made bad shots and even took some shots on the other team's goal. It was obvious that there was no heart or passion in their efforts. It's hard to understand that a team would try to lose a game, and I'm sure if these girls could do it over, they would all make some different choices.

When you hear about a team that tries to lose on purpose, you probably don't understand it. You may even think that you would never do anything like that. And yet, in our spiritual lives we often settle for defeated living instead of fighting hard for the victory.

Consider the following:

- *What are some things that you do and say that leans more toward spiritual defeat than spiritual victory?*
- *What areas of your life are you making choices that don't set you up for a win?*
- *Does your attitude tell people that you are planning to settle for loss when you could be reaching for victory? Explain.*

These are good questions that we need to consider. Look at what 1 John 5:4-5 says: "... whatever has been born of God conquers the world. This is the victory that has conquered the world: our faith. And who is the one who conquers the world but the one who believes that Jesus is the Son of God?" We have victory through our faith in Christ Jesus. That, ladies, is awesome.

Last week we talked about the reality of spiritual warfare. Even though we have a real Enemy, we can't let the fear of facing him keep us from going for victory! These next few days we will walk through some specific things you can do to start living in victory in all of your life. We must be women who GO FOR IT and who don't settle for less than all that God has for us!

DAY 1

Start Small

If you are faithful in little things, you will be faithful in large ones. But if you are dishonest in little things, you won't be honest with greater responsibilities. Luke 16:10 (NLT)

Consider the following statement:

You can live victoriously because of Christ's work on the cross.

Maybe you wholeheartedly agree with that sentence. Perhaps you think it is only true when you've been going to church a lot and making good choices. Or maybe, you think you're way too far gone to ever truly live a life of victory.

The Enemy would like nothing more than for us to live in shame and defeat in this life. But girls, when we live like that, we are completely ineffective for God's kingdom. There are too many people today who wear the Christian label yet live completely defeated lives. They live in sin and shame, not flourishing and living victoriously. And as believers, we *are* victorious. Not because of anything we have done, but simply because we trust that Jesus has won the victory for us.

We all have to start somewhere on the road to living victoriously, so don't be afraid to start small. If you feel defeated in a certain area of your life, set goals for yourself and strive to overcome them. For example, if you feel like you just can't overcome a certain sin struggle, set a goal to avoid environments where that sin is most tempting. After consistently achieving your "little win," you will notice growth, and it will be easier to go for bigger goals. So, going back to the earlier example, perhaps a "bigger goal" would be to tell a trusted mentor, youth leader, or parent about the struggle, and ask them to hold you accountable. Remember: when you accept Christ as Savior and follow Him, you already have victory. But to live the *even more* life that He desires for us, we have to choose to *live* victoriously every single day. Setting goals for ourselves can help us in that process.

Take time to celebrate the small things. There is no such thing as an insignificant win when you're moving forward and allowing the Holy Spirit to transform your life from the inside out. As Luke 16:10 says, "Whoever is faithful in very little is also faithful in much." There's nothing insignificant in that! Through the grace and guidance of God in our lives, we can live victoriously. That doesn't mean we will be completely perfect all the time—far from it. But it does mean that, by finding victory in small goals, we can better experience the life that God wants us to live, and that is something worth celebrating.

We want to be clear: setting goals is good, but you can't find true victory in your works. Only through Christ working on your heart and in your life can you live victoriously on this earth. So, how do you allow Christ to work in your life? By spending time with Him. As one of your goals, decide on a consistent time and place to meet with the Lord every day. Maybe you will wake up just 10 minutes earlier than normal to spend time in His Word. Be consistent, and you'll see a difference in your life. We often hear people say that they wish they had more time to spend with Jesus, but we will only have time when we decide that He is worthy of our time. We can't be the women that He wants us to be apart from spending time with Him, in His Word and in prayer.

It's time to put action to our words. We've heard it said that it takes approximately 21 days to create a new habit. Start small and set goals. Prioritize God and spend time with Him. From these little goals, you will see a big change in your desires and actions.

Quit settling for average or status quo. And while you are at it, stop giving yourself excuses to quit before you even begin! If you're looking for an excuse, you'll find one every time.

"No, in all these things we are more than victorious through Him who loved us."
ROMANS 8:37

PRACTICE (JOURNAL & PRAY)

♦ In your journal, answer the following questions.

  ♦ *Are you known as a girl who always gives up or has an excuse for not finishing what you start? Explain.*

  ♦ *Where do you need victory in your life? In what areas are you struggling?*

♦ Take some time to confess your areas of struggle to God. Thank Him for sending Jesus to give you ultimate victory over your sin and ask Him to help you live victoriously in every area of your life. Ask the Holy Spirit to transform your character to be more like Christ.

LINGER

♦ Reread: Luke 16:10
♦ Dwell: Romans 8:37
♦ Memorize: Luke 16:10A

PROCEED

Use this section to keep moving forward as you apply the lesson to your daily life. Talk about it with someone you trust who can help you walk this spiritual journey with victory.

♦ Discuss the questions you worked through in the "Practice" section.

♦ Set goals together. If we don't verbalize our goals/commitments, there's no accountability in reaching them and we give up a lot easier.

♦ Spend some time celebrating the little victories together. Encourage each other by the ways you've seen spiritual growth in your friend.

And if it is evil in your eyes to serve the Lord, choose this day whom you will serve, whether the gods your fathers served in the region beyond the River, or the gods of the Amorites in whose land you dwell. But as for me and my house, we will serve the Lord. Joshua 24:15 (ESV)

Who is in control of a car when it's moving? Whether you're a licensed driver or not, the answer to that question is obvious: duh, it's the person driving. A car is controlled by the driver, and it will stay on the road or drive off in a ditch according to the choices the driver makes.

This week we are talking about living victoriously, and today our focus is on our drivers—not literal chauffeurs, but the spiritual "drivers" of your life. Compare your life to a car. Spiritually speaking, who is driving your life? Who is in control on a daily basis?

Every day when you wake up, someone has the power over your life. If you're a believer in Jesus Christ, then there are only two choices of drivers—you or the Holy Spirit. When you asked Jesus into your heart, the Holy Spirit took up residence in your life, BUT you still get to choose whether or not to give Him complete control over your thoughts, actions, and words.

Your flesh fights to get its way. Think about those times when you feel compelled to do something because you want to, even though it isn't a godly choice—that's your flesh. Now, you understand what we are talking about.

Joshua 24:15 gives great advice for being proactive on this control issue. Check it out: "...choose *THIS* day whom you will serve, whether the gods your fathers served in the region beyond the River, or the gods of the Amorites in whose land you dwell. But as for me and my house, we will serve the LORD" (ESV). Did you get that? Every single day we have a choice to make. Will we serve other gods (including ourselves), or will we serve the Lord? The one that we serve ultimately has control over our lives, so we must choose wisely.

Be careful not to confuse the choice of whom we will serve with the choice to allow Jesus to save us from our sin. Those are two separate (yet connected) choices. Yes, the choice of whom we will serve will be influenced by our salvation, but we must still choose to give control to God of every aspect of our lives. Notice that the passage says, "this day." This very day—and every day—we must choose to give God control. Why? Because He asks us to give Him control, and it is for our best.

Think about the days that you have "blown it" spiritually. Those days—you tried to drive your own life. On your own, you will drive yourself toward sin, because that is the normal human tendency. But when you step back and let Christ take control, your "car" will drive in the route of righteousness. If you aren't sure who is in control, consider this: when you're influenced by the flesh, your mind-set is *I deserve it all.* When you're influenced by the Spirit, your mind-set is *I surrender all.* When you look at your recent words and actions, it is probably clear which of these mind-sets you're living under. The evidence doesn't lie or trick us. When we exhibit the fruit of the Spirit, we are under His power. When we exhibit the fruit of the flesh, we are in the driver's seat.

Choose daily to give God the control of your life and heart, and then you can enjoy and celebrate the victories!

PRACTICE-JOURNAL & PRAYER

◆ In your journal, write down your answers to the following questions.
  ◆ *Who is in control of your life more often—you or the Holy Spirit? Explain your answer.*
  ◆ *What evidence can you see in your life when you are in control? When God is in control? How do you know?*
◆ Spend some time in prayer, confessing the times when you find yourself taking charge and not living surrendered. Ask God to make you sensitive to those times so you can give control back over to the Lord intentionally throughout your day. Thank Him for caring enough about you to be involved in your daily life.

LINGER

◆ Reread: Joshua 24:15
◆ Dwell: Romans 6:16
◆ Memorize: Joshua 24:15

PROCEED

Use this section to keep moving forward as you apply the lesson to your daily life. Talk about it with someone you trust who can help you walk this spiritual journey with victory.

◆ Romans 6:16 says that you are slaves to the one you obey. What does it look like to be a slave to yourself? What does it look like to be a slave to God?
◆ Discuss the implications of you being in control instead of the Holy Spirit.
◆ Hold each other accountable this week to declaring whom you will serve each day.

DAY 3

It's Not About You

Then Jesus said to His disciples, "If anyone wants to come with Me, he must deny himself, take up his cross, and follow Me."
Matthew 16:24

At the 2015 Grammy® Awards, Kanye West stormed the stage (yet another time) to interrupt an artist's acceptance speech for album of the year. You may remember that this exact same thing happened to poor Taylor Swift back in 2009 at the MTV Video Music Awards©. When I saw this happen, I thought, *I cannot believe this dude! Who does he think he is?* Sadly, we see countless artists and celebrities who think that life is all about them. But let's be honest, we aren't all that different.

Lots of people—both believers and non-believers alike—think life is all about them. As believers, we're not immune to pride. It's easy to revert back to the flesh and believe the world revolves around us.

Jesus, however, presents a different argument about what our lives should be focused on. In Matthew 16:24, He said, "If anyone wants to come with Me, he must deny himself, take up his cross, and follow Me." Jesus presented us with a few things that we must do as people who claim to be Christians. These aren't suggestions for followers of Jesus; they are non-negotiables. We are told three things: deny ourselves, take up our crosses, and follow Jesus.

So, let's break down that first command. What does it mean to "deny" ourselves? Simply put, it's to say no to ourselves and yes to

God. Jesus is not saying to forgo earthly possessions or ignore this world, but to die to our selfish ambitions and live for Him instead.

It's a choice that we have to make daily. Self-denial is such a foreign concept in our world today. We live in a culture that screams *it's all about you* and *do what makes you happy*, so this verse is extremely counter cultural. But it's imperative for us to grasp this concept of denying ourselves if we want even more of what He has for us.

Jesus took the idea of self-denial one step further in His next command: take up your cross. In Jesus' day, the cross was a symbol for death. By saying this, Jesus was telling us that as followers of Christ, we must die to our ambitions. Our lives will no longer revolve around our own agendas, but instead focus on His plan for our lives that leads us to the final command Jesus gave us: follow. It's that simple. As believers, we live for Christ, not for ourselves.

We must ask Jesus to help us break free from our selfishness and pride that we are all guilty of possessing. When we live humbly, laying aside our own selfish gain, this is proof to a lost world that Jesus has worked in our hearts and lives. The new longing of our hearts is to do what He desires for us and not what we desire. We give up the starring role with the limelight on us, and, instead, place Him in that position of honor.

As we pursue even more of what He has for our lives, we must possess the mind-set that says *it's not about me*. Let's be mindful of ways to make our lives all about Him. Think of the illustration of a traffic sign with a huge arrow telling you which exit to take or the way to go. It's as if we are a giant arrow pointing straight at Him! That's our role here on earth. We're cast to play a part in His story of redemption and to help tell that story to the world. When He's in control and in the driver's seat of our lives, there's no better place to be!

PRACTICE (JOURNAL & PRAY)

- In your journal, write down your answer to the following question.
  - *How have you been guilty of making this life all about you?*
- Take some time to examine your heart. Confess to the Lord any selfish agenda that has become a priority over following God.
- Pray for a hunger for His plan over your own. Remember, your life should be an arrow that points to Him and shows others the way to Him. May our lives clearly communicate who we follow to this lost world.

LINGER

- Reread: Matthew 6:24
- Dwell: Mark 14:36 (NLT)
- Memorize: Proverbs 16:3

PROCEED

Use this section to keep moving forward as you apply the lesson to your daily life. Talk about it with someone you trust who can help you walk this spiritual journey with victory.

- Discuss specific ways you can deny yourself this week. Where and when are you most vulnerable to getting prideful? What will you do when pride tries to rear up in you?
- Discuss the importance of living in a manner that displays to the world that our lives are about God, not ourselves. Again, this is a struggle for most believers to surrender to His will for our lives. Hold each other accountable to live for Christ, and thus live victoriously.

Tangled Up

Therefore, since we are surrounded by such a great cloud of witnesses, let us throw off everything that hinders and the sin that so easily entangles. And let us run with perseverance the race marked out for us, fixing our eyes on Jesus, the pioneer and perfecter of faith. For the joy set before him he endured the cross, scorning its shame, and sat down at the right hand of the throne of God. Hebrews 12:1-2 (NIV)

I've seen quite a few movies that focus on the sport of running. These films focus on runners who push, fight, work, and struggle to prepare for a race. These runners' whole lives revolve around working to gain victory when crossing the finish line. Now, some of us are definitely not runners—some of us don't even like to run. But that doesn't mean we can't relate. In our quest to live in victory, we need dedication, focus, and perseverance to overcome challenges and become the victors that God has called us to be.

In Hebrews 12:1-2, we are challenged to think like runners and make some changes in our lives that will enable us to be victorious. Today, let's just focus on one aspect of this passage—"let us throw off everything that hinders and the sin that so easily entangles." It doesn't take a rocket scientist to realize that if you want to be victorious as

a runner, you need to get rid of things that hinder or entangle you. Think about how defeating it is when you're running and have extra weight on you or get tripped by something. In the same way, sin makes our efforts to follow God so much more difficult.

It can be exhausting and distracting when you constantly struggle with a sin. As you know from our week studying spiritual warfare, it is Satan's goal to keep us wrapped in our sin. Our Enemy is aware of the sins that most easily entangle us, and he is always happy to hit us with temptation in our weakest areas.

So, how can you "throw off" the sin that you struggle with? Well, let's be real. The reason why you sin is because you like it for some reason. Either you enjoy the way it makes you feel, love the escape it offers, or like the control it gives you. You wouldn't choose the sin if it didn't do something for you. That means the first step to getting victory over that sin is to change the way you think about it. You have to start hating your sin the way that God hates it. Instead of thinking about what you like about the sin, think about what you hate about it—the way you feel later, the danger to your reputation or influence, or the consequence of your sin breaking your fellowship with God. It's even helpful to simply recognize that you lose the race every time you give in to your sinful, selfish desires. When you think about sin differently, you will be less attracted to it.

Next, treat sin differently. Think about it: you generally don't spend time with something that you hate. You don't hang out with it; you don't spend money to bring it into your life; you have nothing to do with it. If you truly hate the sin that entangles your life—or even if you simply want to get to the point of hating your sin—then you must begin to treat it differently. Avoid places that cause you to sin. Steer clear of people that cause you to sin. Don't watch movies that tempt you to live in a way that doesn't honor Christ. Basically, stop putting yourself in the position to encounter the sin that keeps you from running the race in victory. Pray that God will change the way you feel about your sin until you no longer have the desire to do it at all. Ask God to help you feel the way that He does about sin, and keep resisting it until your heart actually changes. That's a VICTORY!

PRACTICE (JOURNAL & PRAY)

◆ Answer the following questions in your journal.
   ◆ *What sins do you find yourself committing over and over?*
   ◆ *How does it make you feel when you have to confess the same thing time and again?*
   ◆ *What are the consequences of being entangled in your sin?*
   ◆ *What are the things that attract you to your sin?*

◆ Be honest with God. Let Him know how bad you feel that you are attracted to sin that is not part of His plans for your life. Ask the Lord to change your heart about each sin you've listed, and to see these sins like God does—to hate the sin and to have the strength to avoid situations that bring the sins into your life.

LINGER

◆ Reread: Hebrews 12:1-2
◆ Dwell: Hebrews 12:1
◆ Memorize: 2 Corinthians 10:5B

PROCEED

Use this section to keep moving forward as you apply the lesson to your daily life. Talk about it with someone you trust who can help you walk this spiritual journey with victory.

◆ Read 2 Corinthians 10:5b and discuss how applying this verse to your life when struggling with sin can take away the power and attraction it has for you. When you can stop sin while it is still a thought, you will prevent it from becoming an action.

◆ Pray for each other as you face and fight against your sin. Hold each other accountable and encourage each other in the fight.

Par-tay!

But thanks be to God, who gives us the victory through our Lord Jesus Christ! 1 Corinthians 15:57

I've always loved watching celebration footage after a good game—like after the Super Bowl or World Series. Regardless of who wins, it's fun to see the celebration. As the confetti flies and family members storm the field, there's always that one crazy player who screams to the camera, "I'm going to Disney World!" Then, all the players jump on each other and express their gratitude to coaches. There is just something joyful about watching as they celebrate together. All of the hard work and long hours that they put in together as a team have paid off.

It reminds me of the kind of celebration we should be having in the church. If we are to live this life in victory and power, we should constantly be celebrating what God is doing in and through our lives. Even when life is hard, it is always good because of Jesus! He is our hope and peace—the only constant, secure, and truly good thing in our lives. Through the victories of our spiritual walk, celebration is necessary!

As we said, life will be hard. Jesus even promises us that in John 16:33: "I have told you these things, so that in me you may have peace. In this world you will have trouble. But take heart! I have

overcome the world." He doesn't promise that this life is going to be easy, but He does remind us that He has already overcome this world. He has overcome, and His victory is a WIN for us! At the end of the day, we are on the winning team. All of our earthly struggles with sin can be overcome in the name of Jesus. Can I get an amen?

So girls, it's time to stop wallowing in our self-pity and excuses, and stand up in Jesus' name! As we take the necessary steps to be more like Jesus in our spiritual walks, we need to remember to stop and celebrate those areas of improvement. We need to spend time thanking God for helping us succeed and for shaping us to look more like Him. As 1 Corinthians 15:57 says, "But thanks be to God, who gives us the victory through our Lord Jesus Christ!"

Jesus didn't save us so we could live timid lives, in bondage to sin, our flesh, and our pasts. He died to give us LIFE in abundance! John 10:10 says "...I came so they can have real and eternal life, more and better life than they ever dreamed of" (MSG). We need to stop settling for less in our lives, because Jesus wants to give us a life of abundance in Him—a life of victory and celebration, not defeat. As the old hymn says "Because He lives I can face tomorrow" (Bill and Gloria Gaither, 1971). Our victory celebration is set in the hope that Jesus has overcome.

So, as we experience those small and large victories in our lives, let's celebrate!

PRACTICE (JOURNAL & PRAY)

- In your journal, answer the following questions.
  - *How can you be thankful for the good and the bad in your life?*
  - *Do you live with a spirit of celebration over the work Christ has done in your life? Why or why not?*
- Spend some time today in prayer, thanking Jesus for the hope that you've found in Him. Thank Him that He works all things for good in our lives, as Romans 8:28 says.

LINGER

- Reread: 1 Corinthians 15:57
- Dwell: John 10:10
- Memorize: Romans 8:28

PROCEED

Use this section to keep moving forward as you apply the lesson to your daily life. Talk about it with someone you trust who can help you walk this spiritual journey with victory.

- Make a list of victories you can celebrate together. Include ways that God has helped you in your struggles and the fact that Christ has overcome this world.
- It's vital for us to surround ourselves with like-minded people in this journey—those who are also pursuing Christ, who will be there for the good and bad, and who will speak Truth into your life when you need it the most. These are also the people who are there to encourage and celebrate the victories with you. As you close today, take a few minutes to celebrate all that God has done in your lives.

FREED UP

———————◆———————

...efore, if the Son sets you free,
you really will be free.

JOHN 8:36

I was recently at an event where I heard something shocking. I knew that human trafficking is a horrible issue, but I learned that there are more slaves in our world now than ever before. That's shocking, sad, and terrible. I also learned more about the life conditions of those in slavery, and it broke my heart. Being aware of the human trafficking problem in our world today should move us to action, and I hope it does. It should also make us more aware of the idea of slavery.

It's heartbreaking to think about anyone being trapped in slavery or bondage physically, yet we often allow ourselves to remain enslaved to sin in our daily lives. As we consider the issue of slavery in relation to what we've been studying these past few weeks, we come to another proof—and it's the opposite of slavery. Evidence that we are living an *even more* life in Christ is by an understanding and acceptance of the freedom we have in Jesus.

Over the next five days, you will explore some different aspects of living in freedom and begin to discover areas in your life where you are subjecting yourself to slavery. You may be thinking that you aren't a slave to anything and that no one would willingly allow themselves to be a slave, but look at what Galatians 4:8-9 says: "Formerly, when you did not know God, you were enslaved to those that by nature are not gods. But now that you have come to know God, or rather to be known by God, how can you turn back again to the weak and worthless elementary principles of the world, whose slaves you want to be once more?" When we allow ourselves to be influenced by the weak principles of the world, we quickly become slaves to the world's lies. Many of us are slaves to the expectations of media or of peers. We are slaves to maintaining a certain image or stereotype of who we should be based on the ideas of others. Wow, that's tough to hear! God does not want us to be enslaved to anything or anyone. He wants His children to only care about what He thinks of them. When we see ourselves through His eyes, we find freedom and rest.

Second Corinthians 3:17-18 stresses that we are free in Christ and are being transformed, and John 8:36 clearly states that we are free. That means we don't have to be slaves to the bondage of this world. When we truly understand God's view of us, we will be empowered to live in freedom. It's a process, but it's definitely worth the time and effort! Come on, let's set some more captives free this week.

Break Free

It is for freedom that Christ has set us free. Stand firm, then, and do not let yourselves be burdened again by a yoke of slavery.
Galatians 5:1 (NIV)

Consider what your life would look like if you were a slave. You may automatically think back to your history class when you learned about the generations of lives that were affected by slavery throughout history. But did you know that there are approximately 36 million slaves living in bondage around the globe today? [3] In fact, there are more slaves in the world right now than at any other time in history. Let that sink in for a minute. Today, in the 21st century, there are more slaves being oppressed, used, and held captive than at ANY other time in history. These slaves have been taken from their families and forced to work tirelessly, under the control of another human being. They are given no reprieve, and are used for the selfish gain of others.

Oppressed. Depressed. Hopeless. Fearful. No self-worth or dignity. Pain, both physically and emotionally. These are just a few words that express the reality of those who are enslaved. Even if you are technically a free human, you could experience slavery in a spiritual

sense. Maybe you are enslaved to your fear or shame. Maybe you are enslaved to others' expectations of you.

In Galatians 5:1, Paul is talking to believers, not to actual slaves, about being set free. Check out his challenge to us: "...do not let yourselves be burdened again by a yoke of slavery." The phrase "burdened again by a yoke of slavery" may sound confusing, but it is actually a helpful visual illustration. Have you ever been to a farm or seen a cow with a yoke over its neck? If you don't know what a yoke is, it was a common tool for farmers before heavy machinery was used on farms. It's essentially a wooden frame or bar that fits across the back of the animal's neck so that it could pull or move something heavy. Paul used the visual of a yoke to illustrate the point that because of Jesus Christ, believers no longer have to carry the load of guilt and oppression as if we were still enslaved to our sins. We can break free.

It's likely that we will never wear a yoke or experience the nightmare of slavery. But let's be honest, our lives can exhibit some of the characteristics of slavery both spiritually and emotionally, even if we're believers in Jesus Christ. There are countless Christians today who are living their lives burdened by a yoke of slavery. They walk around with their heads hanging low, claiming the label of Christian without truly allowing the transforming power of Jesus Christ to bring freedom to the places where they're in bondage. People in that place are missing out on the abundant life that Jesus offers. Jesus came to remove the yoke of slavery from our lives, to redeem us, and to set us FREE. He came to release us from this bondage of sin that we carry around. He also lifts us from our efforts to be perfect or please others. He saw us in our sin, and He loved us enough to save us. He rescued us from a life of emotional and spiritual slavery and offers us the opportunity to experience true freedom and abundant life!

If you were removed from slavery, why on earth would you choose to go back to that kind of oppressive life? As believers, why would we EVER choose to go back to our lives before Christ? Psalm 103:12 says, "As far as the east is from the west, so far has he removed our transgressions from us." We don't have to live like a slave. We don't have to lock things up in the vault of our souls. We need to allow Jesus to come in to those secret places and bring hope and healing so we can truly experience a life of freedom. Through the blood of Jesus

Christ, we've been set free! But freedom is a choice we have to make for ourselves.

If you're struggling with some of the "junk" in your life that you can't seem to get over, check out our first book *Salvaging My Identity*. It's a 40-day experience that walks you through eight "projects." Each project addresses five areas of "junk" that need to be dealt with in the salvaging process. Because, as we've covered today, we all have places in our hearts that need some serious restoring. Through God restoring our souls and reminding us of who we are in Him, we can become bold, confident women of God. When we live in freedom, we let go of things that hinder us from doing what God has created us to do—to proclaim His truth or hope and freedom to the world.

But it's a choice that you have to make. Are you going to live and walk in freedom, able to shine the light of Jesus to this dark world? Or will you pick up your yoke of slavery and continue to carry it on your back despite the freedom you have in Christ?

Thank you, Jesus, that You came and died so that we can experience true and complete freedom from our sin and shame!

Now the Lord is the Spirit, and where the Spirit of the Lord is, there is freedom. We all, with unveiled faces, are looking as in a mirror at the glory of the Lord and are being transformed into the same image from glory to glory; this is from the Lord who is the Spirit.

2 CORINTHIANS 3:17-18

PRACTICE (JOURNAL & PRAY)

◆ In your journal, write down your answer to the following question:.
  ◆ *What yoke of slavery are you most tempted to cling to?*
  ◆ *What is your motivation to refuse the yoke of slavery?*
◆ Be honest with the Lord today about areas of your life where you still live as a slave. Thank Him for the freedom you have through Jesus. Ask Him to help you remember that you are free of your sin and shame and to bring healing and restoration to your life.

LINGER

◆ Reread: Galatians 5:1
◆ Dwell: Galatians 4:4-7
◆ Memorize: Psalm 103:12

PROCEED

Use this section to keep moving forward as you apply the lesson to your daily life. Talk about it with someone you trust who can help you walk this spiritual journey with victory.

◆ Discuss responses to the question in the "Practice" section.
◆ Only when we find freedom in Christ can we help others find freedom as well. Discuss ways to bring aid to the slavery crisis. Check out some of the local and global ministries that are fighting human trafficking.

Slave to Christ = Freedom

Don't you know that if you offer yourselves to someone as obedient slaves, you are slaves of that one you obey—either of sin leading to death or of obedience leading to righteousness?
Romans 6:16

A popular late night show used to have a segment called "Things That Make You Go Hmm." It focused on bringing up random but well known terms and phrases that seem to contradict themselves. For instance, *jumbo shrimp, living dead, open secret, seriously funny, bitter sweet,* and *larger half.* The host would read the terms and stress the different aspects, asking things like, "How can one half be larger than the other?" It was really funny. The more I watched this segment, the more I began to notice the use of incredibly ironic terms in my own daily interactions.

Today as we continue our discovery of living in freedom, it may seem ironic to learn that in order to be free, we need to be a slave. I know, crazy! But this truth is grounded in the Word of God. When we get past the irony, we'll see that there is a lot of freedom in being a slave, as long as you are a slave to the right Master.

Romans 6:16 says, "Don't you know that if you offer yourselves to someone as obedient slaves, you are slaves of that one you

obey—either of sin leading to death or of obedience leading to righteousness?" Notice that we are slaves to the one we obey. In other words, we are all slaves to someone or something, because we all obey someone or something. According to the Bible, we are either a slave to sin or to righteousness. Those who are slaves to sin are heading in the direction of death, but those who are slaves to righteousness are on the path to life. The key is that we need to choose what we obey and serve.

As we learned about yesterday, when you choose to obey sin, you become a slave to things that will trap you in bondage and keep you from living the life of freedom that God desires for you. Think about a time when you were caught up in some kind of sin. You were driven to continue in the sin by your own desires and may have even felt helpless or powerless to resist. The more you gave in to the sin, the harder it was to break free from it. It's a vicious cycle that is designed by the Enemy to keep you enslaved.

Now, think about the flip side. What happens when you obey the Word of God and follow the leadership of the Holy Spirit? Every victory or step of obedience transforms you more to the image of Christ. When you are a "slave to righteousness," you become stronger and tougher, and you are better able to stand against the traps of the Enemy. Victory leads to victory, because once you get a taste of what living in freedom is like, then being a slave to sin will seem completely unappealing.

So, what exactly does it mean to be a slave to righteousness? It means you are actively pursuing Christ and working to obey Him in every avenue of your life. Your life becomes less about you and more about serving God and making His name known. When you are a slave to righteousness, your entire identity is based on serving your Master. When you choose to become a slave to Jesus, you are choosing obedience that leads to righteousness, and that life is all about freedom—NO bondage, just freedom.

PRACTICE (JOURNAL & PRAY)

◆ Journal about the ways you've allowed yourself to be a slave to sin instead of righteousness. Why are you choosing to be under the power of sin instead of the Spirit? In what ways can you pursue righteousness in your social life, with your family, in the way you treat your peers, and so forth.

◆ Write Romans 6:16 on your mirror or another place where you can see it every morning. Commit to starting your day by choosing to be a slave to God rather than to sin.

◆ Spend some time in prayer. Confess areas of your life in which you've chosen to be a slave to sin instead of righteousness. Offer yourself to God as a willing slave to Him.

LINGER

◆ Reread: Romans 6:16
◆ Dwell: Romans 8:4-6
◆ Memorize: Romans 6:16

PROCEED

Use this section to keep moving forward as you apply the lesson to your daily life. Talk about it with someone you trust who can help you walk this spiritual journey with victory.

◆ Discuss the most common ways that you tend to be a slave to sin. Talk about how you can help each other be prepared to say no to the sin and yes to the Spirit.

◆ Pray for each other throughout the week to have the strength to pursue righteousness, not sin. Halfway through the week, call or text each other and give an update on how you are doing so far.

DAY 3 — Freedom & Responsibility

What should we say then? Should we continue in sin so that grace may multiply? Absolutely not! How can we who died to sin still live in it? Romans 6:1-2

Grace. This word is really hard for our finite minds to completely understand. According to the ., grace is the "Undeserved acceptance and love received from another, especially the characteristic attitude of God in providing salvation for sinners." [4] As believers in Jesus Christ, we have been given grace through the very life of Jesus Christ. He has given us the gift of freedom and life through the sacrifice He made on the cross.

Having been involved in student ministry for many years, we've seen many students incorrectly use this gift of grace as a "green card" of sorts. They see grace as allowing them to do whatever they want, because they have received grace and forgiveness from God.

Other students we've encountered don't understand grace at all. They try to manipulate rules or situations so they can come as close to the "sin boundary" as possible. For example, we've heard questions such as, *How far is too far with a guy?* These people have probably not experienced the heart transformation that comes when truly understanding God's gift of grace. Those who have experienced the transforming power of grace will not try to figure out how close to the line of sin they can get, but rather flee from it because they've seen the freedom and life that His grace offers.

Whether we're purposefully living in sin or trying to manipulate the gift of grace by creating boundaries, we need to step back and evaluate our hearts because, either way, we don't have a correct view of the gift of grace in our lives. Grace is also not just a means of forgiveness or a free ticket to heaven. Grace sets us apart for holiness. Grace spurs us on to live for God's glory and purposes. The entire direction of our lives change when we experience the goodness of His grace.

Paul addressed this issue in Romans 6:1-2. He said, "...Should we continue in sin so that grace may multiply? Absolutely not! How can we who died to sin still live in it?" He reiterated that believers have died to sin. We have a new nature. However, our new nature in Christ is still housed in sinful flesh. Because of that, we will still struggle and be tempted by sin, but because we've been rescued and redeemed through the blood of Jesus, why on earth would we consciously choose to go on living in sin? In Romans 12:9 Paul also challenged believers that our "love must be without hypocrisy. Detest evil; cling to what is good." In other words, quit going back and forth between worldliness and godliness. Choose to live in the grace that Christ offers.

Our lives must look different from the world if we are choosing to live in the grace and freedom of Jesus Christ. If we claim the label of Christian, but our lives don't mirror Christ, how can we influence others for God? Philippians 2:14-15 explains why living a life of grace and freedom is critical in our world today: "Do everything without grumbling and arguing, so that you may be blameless and pure, children of God who are faultless in a crooked and perverted generation, among whom you shine like stars in the world." Again, this grace is a remarkable gift! People will see the freedom and joy in our lives due to the gift of grace from Jesus, and they will want to experience it as well.

PRACTICE (JOURNAL & PRAY)

- In your journal, write down your answers to the following questions.
  - *How would you define grace?*
  - *Have you found yourself guilty of using or abusing this beautiful and freeing gift? Explain.*
  - *How have you been straddling the fence between godliness and worldliness?*
- Take some time to pray, asking God to forgive you for abusing His gift of grace. Thank Him for the grace He offers.

LINGER

- Reread: Romans 6:1-2
- Dwell: Romans 6:1-14
- Memorize: Philippians 2:14-15

PROCEED

Use this section to keep moving forward as you apply the lesson to your daily life. Talk about it with someone you trust who can help you walk this spiritual journey with victory.

- Discuss what grace means to you. Talk through the areas you struggle with when it come to freedom and responsibility.
- Discuss how you can lead your friends and peers to live boldly, taking a stand for godliness and holiness. How can you be responsible with the gift of grace you've been given?

DAY 4

Wise Thing?

For you were called to be free, brothers; only don't use this freedom as an opportunity for the flesh, but serve one another through love. Galatians 5:13

"Everything is permissible for me," but not everything is helpful. "Everything is permissible for me," but I will not be brought under the control of anything. 1 Corinthians 6:12

What happens when you get the right answer to the wrong question?

One time I was in an unfamiliar place, and I was struggling to find the church where I was scheduled to speak. My cell service was spotty and unreliable, so I did the old-fashioned thing and stopped to ask for directions. When I asked if I was on the road to the First Baptist Church, the man affirmed I was heading in the right direction. He told me to continue driving for about three more miles, then I would see the church on the right.

Several minutes later, I pulled into an empty parking lot and wondered where everyone was. I pulled out my event information notes and looked at the name of the church I was scheduled to speak at. Then I looked at the sign of the church and noticed my mistake. I was at the First Baptist Church, but I was in the wrong town! I had gotten the right answer, but had asked the wrong question. And the results were not good!

Has anything like that ever happened to you? We spend way too much time asking the wrong questions to guide our lives. We like to ask things like, *How much questionable stuff does a movie need to have to keep me from going?* or *Which cuss words are the worst for me to say?* But we don't need another do or don't list—that's not what the Christian life is about. It is about freedom, life, joy, and peace that can only be found by fully following God.

What if we learned to ask one simple question to give us direction and help us live in freedom? Sounds great, right? Here's what we should be asking: *What is the wise thing to do?* It's as simple as that. Galatians 5:13 and 1 Corinthians 6:12 reinforce the idea that we should concern ourselves with the pursuit of wisdom. In Galatians, we see that when we ask the wrong questions, we are feeding our flesh. We're trying to live as the world without stepping too far over the line, but that is NOT wise living. Wise living is seeking the Lord in all things. It is desperately trying to make choices that please and honor Him, even if they aren't the popular things to do.

The passage in 1 Corinthians says, "'Everything is permissible for me,' but not everything is helpful. 'Everything is permissible for me,' but I will not be brought under the control of anything." It's warning us that choosing unwise things will put us under their control. Even though God gives us free will to make our own choices, as believers, we should aim to choose things that glorify God and help us live the life He has called us to.

The next time you're faced with a hard choice, remember to ask the one, simple question: *what is the wise thing to do?* Instead of trying to focus on how much like the world you can be, you start being more concerned with how much like Jesus you can be. That will make a HUGE difference in the way you live your life and the choices you make because when we get the right answer to the wrong question, we still end up in the wrong place.

PRACTICE (JOURNAL & PRAY)

◆ In your journal, answer the following questions.
   ◆ *What are some of the wrong questions you've been using to guide your decision making?*
   ◆ *How does asking the right question change your focus?*
   ◆ *Where does your focus need to be in order to live in freedom?*
◆ List some areas of your life where you need God's wisdom and guidance.
◆ Spend a few minutes in prayer, confessing to God the times you've had the wrong focus. Ask for His wisdom and guidance in every area of your life.

LINGER

◆ Reread: 1 Corinthians 6:12
◆ Dwell: James 1:5
◆ Memorize: Galatians 5:13

PROCEED

Use this section to keep moving forward as you apply the lesson to your daily life. Talk about it with someone you trust who can help you walk this spiritual journey with victory.

◆ Discuss the situations in your life that you need wisdom in right now.
◆ Talk about what James 1:5 says about wisdom and where you can get it.
◆ This week, hold each other accountable to asking the right questions and living in freedom.

The Spirit of the Lord God is on Me, because the Lord has anointed Me to bring good news to the poor. He has sent Me to heal the brokenhearted, to proclaim liberty to the captives and freedom to the prisoners. Isaiah 61:1

When we experience true freedom through Jesus Christ, our excitement and joy over the work He has done in our lives will be contagious to those we encounter on a daily basis.

I absolutely love the story in John 4 of Jesus' encounter with the woman at the well and how it illustrates this evidence that we're going to talk about today. You will definitely need to go back and reread this passage, but here's the abbreviated version: Jesus had been traveling for a while heading from Judea to Galilee. On this particular day, He stopped in the town of Sychar in Samaria, which was actually quite unusual because Jews and Samaritans didn't interact in those days. When most Jews traveled that direction, they would go around Samaria to avoid contact with the Samaritan people. Jesus arrived in the town, and He sat down to rest by a well. While resting, a woman came to the well where she had a life-changing conversation with Jesus. She came to the well seeking water, but Jesus offered her living water.

Then, Jesus told her to go get her husband. In that moment, she realized that He knew a lot more about her than she wanted Him to

know. He knew that she'd had five husbands and that the man she was living with currently wasn't her husband. Jesus extended His grace to her His grace, and she ran back to town to tell everyone about the man she encountered. She told them that they needed to meet Him, too. So they did. In John 4:39 we see that "Many of the Samaritans from that town believed in Him because of the woman's testimony, 'he told me everything I ever did.'"

Much like today, people knew about the woman and her reputation. She had a past like many do. But after her encounter with Jesus, she wanted others to experience her same excitement in discovering the Messiah. She found true freedom and felt liberated to go and share it. She wanted others to have it too! But notice that she had to find freedom first before she could share freedom with anyone else.

When we are truly freed from our sin and liberated to live the abundant life that Jesus died to give us, our hope and joy will be contagious. In John 7:38, Jesus said, "The one who believes in Me, as the Scripture has said, will have streams of living water flow from deep within him." If we believe in faith, this same "living water" will be found within each of us as well! It will flow from within us, and those around us will take notice.

Like the woman at the well, the freedom that we've found in Jesus will compel us to share about this life-changing experience. Life change for eternity is exciting and should compel us to go out and share! As Peter and John stated in Acts 4:20, "For we are unable to stop speaking about what we have seen and heard." We must be concerned for our loved ones and those around us in order to see freedom happen.

Let's close with this verse from Isaiah 61:1—"The Spirit of the LORD God is on Me, because the Lord has anointed Me to bring good news to the poor. He has sent Me to heal the brokenhearted, to proclaim liberty to the captives and freedom to the prisoners." Make this the cry of your heart, girls.

PRACTICE (JOURNAL & PRAY)

◆ Go back and reread this passage for yourself in John 4:1-38. Then, write your answers to the following questions in your journal.

    ◆ *What are your thoughts about this woman and the guilt and bondage she must have carried around in her life?*

    ◆ *How does your life parallel this woman at the well?*

    ◆ *Have you responded to Jesus' gift of grace? If so, how has the hope and grace found in Christ spurred you on to share this good news with others?*

LINGER

◆ Reread: Isaiah 61:1
◆ Dwell: John 7:38
◆ Memorize: Hebrews 10:24

PROCEED

Use this section to keep moving forward as you apply the lesson to your daily life. Talk about it with someone you trust who can help you walk this spiritual journey with victory.

◆ Reread the John 4 passage again as a group, and discuss the questions from the "Practice" section.

◆ Discuss the power of our testimonies and why it's important to go and tell of what Christ has done in our lives.

◆ Pray for boldness and willingness to share the grace of Jesus with others. Keep each other updated on who you have been sharing with and how it has been going.

PROOF #7

STOP SETTLING

You took off your former way of life, the old self that is corrupted by deceitful desires; you are being renewed in the spirit of your minds; you put on the new self, the one created according to God's likeness in righteousness and purity of the truth.

EPHESIANS 4:22-24

*H*ave you ever noticed that some people in your life are the best gift givers? For me, that person is my sister. I always look forward to birthday or Christmas gifts from her, because she has good taste, knows me well, and loves to shop. These three factors make her the very best at giving gifts. She can always find me something that I will love. Awesome, right?

Imagine if I she gave me an awesome scarf in a great color with cool little pockets on the ends to keep my hands warm. I would probably ooh and ahh over it—especially if the colors just happened to match my favorite football team. Now, let's say one freezing fall night I went to watch my football team play, but I wore some old, thin gloves with holes in them and no scarf. How goofy would that be? Why would I let myself freeze when I have a nice, warm scarf with pockets at home, just waiting to be worn?

That would be totally ridiculous. No one would settle for something that is old and bad when they can have something new and good. And yet, we often do something very similar in our spiritual lives. We live like people with no hope, no power, and no victory, when God has given us new life in Christ. Though we are new creations, we often still live the old way, as sinners who are condemned.

Why would you ever settle for a defeated life when you could be living in the joy of your salvation? It doesn't make sense! It's as crazy as never using a gift, like my hypothetical scarf. God's gift of Jesus and salvation should change your life for the better. Jesus died on the cross so you and I could be free. When we cling to our old lives, we are settling for less.

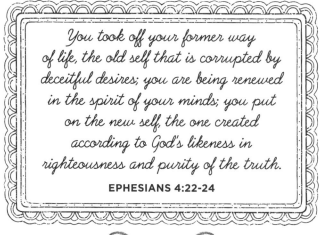

You took off your former way of life, the old self that is corrupted by deceitful desires; you are being renewed in the spirit of your minds; you put on the new self, the one created according to God's likeness in righteousness and purity of the truth.

EPHESIANS 4:22-24

It is ridiculous for us not to put on our new selves. Once we get a taste of what the *even more* life is like, we will refuse to settle for less.

Over the next few days, we will talk more about how you can stop settling and start going for the abundant life that Jesus offers. This is fun stuff, so get ready to clean out the old and start living in the new.

Go Deeper

So then, just as you received Christ Jesus as Lord, continue to live your lives in him. Colossians 2:6 (NIV)

Over the past few years, I have become passionate about two things: digging into the Word and helping young women grasp the goodness of God. To better understand why I am so passionate about these things, you should know a little about me. For far too long, I lived with an average faith, doing the very bare minimum in my walk with Christ. But a few years ago, I was challenged by the women's minister at my church to participate in a year-long Bible study. This study would go through the entire Bible in chronological order. In my 29 years of life, I had never read God's Word all the way through before. To be honest, it had never crossed my mind to even make that a goal, especially since I had two preschoolers at that time. But I decided to make reading through the Bible a goal. I committed to it and did it.

I can't put into words the profound impact that year made on my spiritual life. By the time we completed the study, I was a 30-year-old who had been raised in a Christian home with godly parents and steady church attendance. Still, this was the first time I GOT IT. It was as if a light bulb had gone off in my mind, heart, and soul. It was the first time that the entire Bible—from Genesis to Revelation—was brought to life!

The Lord revealed Himself to me in such a new and fresh way that year, and I believe it was because I dove in head-first. I didn't keep up with my Bible study perfectly—at times I got days or even weeks behind in my reading—but I finished!

So am I saying that the only effective way to go deeper in your relationship with Christ is to read the Bible in its entirety? Not exactly. But studying Scripture is one of the major steps to growing closer to God, along with spending time in prayer, and surrounding yourself with Christian community and accountability. I want to challenge you to spend more time in God's Word, simply because I've personally experienced the power of it. He will reveal Himself through the Bible, you can count on it. In fact, He promises in Scripture that His words never will return void or empty (Isa. 55:11). If you want to truly fall in love with the Word and its Author, then you have to make Bible study a priority.

Girls, if you truly want more of what God has for you in this life, you must leave the floaties in the shallow end of the pool and dive into the deep end. Only when you go "all-in" will you experience the life that God wants for you. Don't be fooled: doing so will radically change your life, but it will be for the better. God Almighty desires for you to choose Him. He wants you to go deeper in your understanding and knowledge of Him. Why? Because He loves you and knows what's best for you. It's time to choose more than status quo Christianity and go deeper in your relationship with Christ.

So, practically speaking, what does it look like to prioritize God's Word in your life? It's not speed reading a verse before bed or crossing off another box on your checklist. It's so much more than that. But that's not to say you have to read an entire chapter in one sitting either. Prioritizing God's Word looks something like this: intentionally setting aside time each day for God's Word, reading through a passage, processing what it says, and asking God to transform your heart as a result of what you've read. Being consistent in the Word creates a healthy dependence on God to get you through each day. Through His Word you'll see how much you need His power, love, and mercy in your life, and this dependence is a good and healthy thing.

In case you were mistaken, living a life that pleases God does not come naturally for us, apart from the Holy Spirit at work in our

lives. Allow the Holy Spirit to speak to your heart through the Word, and then APPLY what the Word says to your life. By doing so, you'll notice that your words, attitude, and the way you love people will greatly change.

Colossians 2:6 is a great summary of the Christian life: "So then, just as you received Christ Jesus as Lord, continue to live your lives in him." Once we receive Jesus as Lord, we must continue to live in Him. It's as simple as that. We're not told that once we receive Jesus as Lord, we must pray occasionally or once we receive Jesus as Lord, we must read the Bible when it's convenient. NO! We are called to live an abundant life in Christ, and to do so, we must go "all-in." God has so much more for us if we're willing to toss the floaties and leave the baby pool. We must trust Him to go deeper!

So dive in to the deep end with the Lord. It's time to leave the mediocre, shallow faith behind and allow God to change us from the inside out!

PRACTICE (JOURNAL & PRAY)

◆ In your journal, write down your answers to the following questions.

    ◆ *What are some ways you can go deeper in your walk with Christ? Be specific.*

    ◆ *Do you need to spend more time in the Word? If so, how can you make sure this time is a priority?*

◆ Pray for God to continue to draw you closer to Him. Repent of time when you've been content with living out a comfortable or selfish faith.

LINGER

◆ Reread: Colossians 2:6
◆ Dwell: Ephesians 4:23-24
◆ Memorize: Colossians 2:6

PROCEED

Use this section to keep moving forward as you apply the lesson to your daily life. Talk about it with someone you trust who can help you walk this spiritual journey with victory.

◆ Discuss the following questions.

    ◆ *Why would you want to stay in the shallow end in your faith? What are you missing out on by staying comfortable and safe?*

    ◆ *Who do you know that has the kind of deeper faith that you want? What does that person do differently than you?*

◆ Consider taking the challenge to read the *One Year Chronological Bible* together. Hold each other accountable along the way. This is a big commitment, but it is so worth the effort. Encourage each other to persevere and really process the Scripture passages.

Step Out

Immediately He made the disciples get into the boat and go ahead of Him to the other side, while He dismissed the crowds. After dismissing the crowds, He went up on the mountain by Himself to pray. When evening came, He was there alone. But the boat was already over a mile from land, battered by the waves, because the wind was against them. Around three in the morning, He came toward them walking on the sea. When the disciples saw Him walking on the sea, they were terrified. "It's a ghost!" they said, and cried out in fear. Immediately Jesus spoke to them. "Have courage! It is I. Don't be afraid." "Lord, if it's You," Peter answered Him, "command me to come to You on the water." "Come!" He said. And climbing out of the boat, Peter started walking on the water and came toward Jesus. But when he saw the strength of the wind, he was afraid. And beginning to sink he cried out, "Lord, save me!" Immediately Jesus reached out His hand, caught hold of him, and said to him, "You of little faith, why did you doubt?" When they got into the boat, the wind ceased. Then those in the boat worshiped Him and said, "Truly You are the Son of God!" Matthew 14:22-33

I have a thing for shoes. I LOVE all kinds of shoes. The more unusual or cool, the better. And if they are on sale, then my day is made! There have been times when I've been lured into a pair of super cool-looking shoes or boots that were on sale for a great price, only to realize later that those shoes were murder to my feet. So, what happens to those shoes? They end up sitting in my closet because I can't stand to wear them if they're uncomfortable.

I know I'm not alone in this. When was the last time you went shopping for clothes or shoes and told the salesperson to find you the most uncomfortable item in the store? Probably never. We are a people who like our comfort and reject those things that cause us pain.

There's nothing wrong with rejecting shoes or clothing that don't fit right or feel uncomfortable, but sometimes our quest to be comfortable spills over into our spiritual lives as well. We avoid anything that might push us out of our comfort zones. By doing so, we miss opportunities to grow in our relationship with Jesus. When we step out in faith, there's no end to the growth we can experience.

Check out what happened to the disciples in the story found in Matthew 14:22-33. Picture the scene: a small boat filled with tired men and a fast approaching storm. The waves began to crash, and the wind began to blow. Then out of the black of night, they saw a man walking toward them on the water—Jesus! And then He spoke to calm them from their fears.

We let fear take over far too often. We look at the "storms" in our lives and become overwhelmed. But notice in Matthew 14 that Jesus was right there in the storm with His disciples. Peter teaches us an important lesson when facing the storms of life—he called out to Jesus and wanted to go where He was. Peter was willing to step out of the comfort of the boat and do something that was beyond his natural ability because He knew the power of the One he was walking toward.

Peter trusted Jesus in the storm, and he WALKED on water! That's HUGE, and it's so challenging to us. It's often easier to stay in the comfort of what we know then to trust God when He tells us to "walk on water" in our own lives. Maybe God's calling you to share His love with others, but you're uncomfortable being vulnerable and open. You don't want to be labeled as weird or different, so you don't talk to that friend or family member that God has laid on your heart. And that, girls, is when comfort takes priority over following God.

God didn't call us to be comfortable; He called us to reach the world with the gospel and to love Him with our hearts, souls, minds, and strength. When we resist stepping out of our comfort zones, we miss out on the growth that comes with pushing ourselves spiritually. By taking the safe route, we're not allowing Him to use us in big and powerful ways for His kingdom. Think about how much that experience on the water benefited Peter and prepared Him for the road ahead. Don't you want that type of experience as well? Step out in faith, trusting that God will protect you and be with you every step of the way.

PRACTICE (JOURNAL & PRAY)

- In your journal, write down your answers to the following questions.
  - *What storms are you riding out right now?*
  - *What evidence do you have that Jesus is with you in the storm? How does that change your perspective on the storm?*
  - *What is keeping you from fully trusting and following God?*
- Ask the Lord to show you areas of your life where you've been living in the comfort zone. Ask God to help you have the confidence and courage to trust His plan and follow Him faithfully. Pray for sensitivity to His leading in your life.

LINGER

- Reread: Matthew 14:22-33
- Dwell: Matthew 14:30-32
- Memorize: Isaiah 41:10

PROCEED

Use this section to keep moving forward as you apply the lesson to your daily life. Talk about it with someone you trust who can help you walk this spiritual journey with victory.

- Discuss how Peter got distracted from walking on water when he focused again on the waves and the storm. Talk through ways that this story relates to your own lives.
- Discuss ways that God has saved you from the storms of life. Point out His faithfulness in each circumstance.
- Talk through the positives that can come from stepping out of your comfort zones and following God.
- Encourage one another to take a step of faith and get out of the boat that represents your comfort zone.

DAY 3 *Push Yourself*

But have nothing to do with irreverent and silly myths. Rather, train yourself in godliness, for the training of the body has a limited benefit, but godliness is beneficial in every way, since it holds promise for the present life and also for the life to come.
1 Timothy 4:7-8

I think at some point in all of our lives, we've pushed really hard to accomplish certain goals. You can push yourself when training for a sport to gain a win or accomplish a better time. You can push yourself academically to get all A's one semester or to gain a GPA that would help you get into your dream college. Pushing ourselves is actually quite common when you think about it. But when was the last time you really pushed yourself spiritually?

As believers, we will always struggle with the desires of our flesh and wrestle with complacency in our spiritual lives. Thus, we must be proactive and strive to be more of who God created us to be. Spiritual complacency is especially typical in America, where being a Christian doesn't appear to require much sacrifice or life change. But girls, here is the deal: we need to be challenged in this thought process because being a Christian actually requires huge sacrifice and complete life-change. Maybe it's time for our hearts and minds to be pushed a bit to get ourselves to the next level spiritually.

No matter if you've been a believer in Jesus Christ for a week or you have known Him since you were 8 years old, none of us have "arrived" spiritually this side of heaven. In order to not settle, we must keep challenging ourselves. How do we go about this? Set a goal to read a book of the Bible each month. Go on a mission trip. Commit to fast one day each month. Start an accountability group or prayer group for you and your friends. Read books that will challenge you to think differently, pray differently, and live differently. Simply put, we push ourselves by prioritizing our relationship with Christ and doing things that will draw us closer to Him.

Just like there are steps to take in order to succeed if you commit to train for a marathon or triathlon, Hebrews 12 reminds us what it takes to be successful in the spiritual race we are running. This passage points out what is required of us to be adequately trained and prepared. We would never practice for a big game or train for a race after that event was over. No way! We train with the anticipation of the race or event, giving our all to obtain victory.

Often during our training, a passion is birthed within us for whatever sport we are involved in. It's like we develop a whole new addiction to that particular event or sport that makes us want more of it! Likewise, we will gain a deeper love for Christ as we train in righteousness. We will experience His goodness and love through spending time in His Word, through being on mission for Him, through the Christian community that we encounter, and our passion for Him will grow!

So, what if we approached our spiritual lives with intensity, doing whatever it took to push us to know God more? We would gain a passion to see Him more clearly and to be a part of His work for the kingdom. That kind of life is victorious and free.

Today's passage in 1 Timothy 4:7-8 challenges us as believers to not get caught up in the petty things of life, but to train ourselves for godliness. Notice the point made that training of our physical bodies only has a limited benefit. But godliness has a benefit for both this life and the next! So, come on, girls, it's time that we pray for a new passion and intensity to be born in our souls. May God's Word come alive to us. May a fire be sparked in us that motivates us to keep pushing our spiritual muscles. Let's run this race with everything we have!

PRACTICE (JOURNAL & PRAY)

- In your journal, write down your answers to the following questions.
    - *When was the last time you "trained in godliness"?*
    - *Think about the intensity and drive we get when we we're fired up about something. What happens? How could your spiritual life be radically changed by a renewed passion for pursuing God and His Word?*
    - *How would you define godliness? Why do you think it takes training to achieve godliness?*

LINGER

- Reread: 1 Timothy 4:7-8
- Dwell: Hebrews 12
- Memorize: Hebrews 12:1-2

PROCEED

Use this section to keep moving forward as you apply the lesson to your daily life. Talk about it with someone you trust who can help you walk this spiritual journey with victory.

- Work together to create a training plan for your spiritual growth. Push yourself to read a few books, memorize Scripture, and serve in your church or community for God's glory. Personalize this plan—only you know what areas you need to strengthen!
- Pray for and encourage each other to run the spiritual race with perseverance and to always keep your eyes on Christ.

Watered Down = Not Attractive

Now may the God of hope fill you with all joy and peace as you believe in Him so that you may overflow with hope by the power of the Holy Spirit. Romans 15:13

I don't know anyone at all who would say they love a watered-down soda. In fact, that just sounds nasty. When a soda has been left sitting for a while and the ice has melted, it loses its flavor and fizz. Yuck! When anything is watered-down, it is weaker, less flavorful, and more likely to be poured out than enjoyed. Who wants something that is watered-down? No one. The same is true spiritually.

If we have "watered-down" spiritual lives, we have settled for below par, ho-hum Christianity. We are selling the world short of seeing the life-changing, life-giving Jesus in us! When our spiritual lives lose flavor and fizz, our faith loses appeal to those around us.

Our prayer is that as you've been walking through this 40 day journey, the Holy Spirit has awakened a fire in your soul to live a bold, passionate, and intentional life for your Savior! There's nothing attractive about a watered down faith to a lost and spiritually dead world. It's like a watered-down soda—just waiting to be poured out and ignored.

Romans 15:13 says, "Now may the God of hope fill you with all joy and peace as you believe in Him so that you may overflow with hope

by the power of the Holy Spirit." Oh, that we would overflow with the hope of Jesus to everyone we encounter! And we can overflow, ladies, because we have experienced the hope of Jesus. But we must LIVE like we possess it. It's time to raise our heads up, roll our shoulders back, and walk in a bold and confident manner in this loud world. It's time to show our faith to those around us. We should strive to have honest and compassionate conversations with people about the love and hope found in a relationship with Christ—the very love and hope that makes up our relationship with Him.

Though we need to approach conversations with kindness, we don't need to be apologetic if our faith is offensive to others. The truth of the Bible is radical, and it should confront those who hear it. For too long believers have stayed back on the sidelines, silent and void of opinion about the issues that matter. Yet, we possess the resurrection power of Christ in us, the hope of eternal life, the answers to the world's most pressing questions. How can we not own this faith and share it with others?

Ladies, hear me today. We need to rise up and live out the hope of our salvation unapologetically because we serve a God who sacrificed His Son for all of humanity—even those who may reject the truth of God that you share. Let's possess and live out bold faith that loves well, forgives all, serves all, and speaks the truth.

Imagine the impact you could have if you stood boldly for truth at your school, on your squads, on your social media, in your home, in your youth ministry and church, in your community, and around the world. Imagine what God could do if you confidently spoke of His work in your life. This world needs to see more bold and passionate believers who live out an attractive faith. Don't settle for a watered-down faith; live so that the whole world can see God's goodness through your life!

PRACTICE (JOURNAL & PRAY)

♦ In your journal, write down your answers to the following questions.

♦ *Do you think your faith is "watered-down" or attractive to those you encounter? Explain.*

♦ *Why is it important to be bold about your relationship with Christ in today's culture?*

♦ *How have you seen God work through your life to bring others to Him? If this hasn't happened to you, why do you think that is?*

♦ Spend a few minutes praying for God to help you boldly and lovingly share Jesus with everyone you encounter. (If a few people in particular come to mind, pray for boldness and opportunity to share with those individuals this week.)

LINGER

♦ Reread: Romans 15:13

♦ Dwell: Philippians 2:15

♦ Memorize: Romans 15:13

PROCEED

Use this section to keep moving forward as you apply the lesson to your daily life. Talk about it with someone you trust who can help you walk this spiritual journey with victory.

♦ Discuss ways you tend to water-down your faith. Talk through the consequences of a watered-down faith.

♦ Pray for each other that God will fire up your passion for Him so that His presence is evident to anyone you come in contact with.

DAY 5

Choose Abundance

The thief does not come except to steal, and to kill, and to destroy. I have come that they may have life, and that they may have it more abundantly. John 10:10 (NKJV)

What's the best choice you've ever made? A certain outfit? Hair style? Friend or boyfriend choice? Have you ever thought about how many different decisions or choices you make every day? Probably zillions (no research here). Some decisions you make without even thinking about them, such as the decision to put toothpaste on your toothbrush or deciding to sit down at the table. Those decisions are obvious because your brain is cool and automatically knows what to do in those situations.

Then there are other choices that require a little more thought, such as deciding your coffee order or what shirt you will wear each day. These decisions, though still small, aren't quite as mindless. But still, the risk involved in these decisions is minimal, so even if you aren't happy with your choice, it doesn't majorly affect your life in the long run.

Then, there are those HUGE decisions, such as deciding what college to go to, who you will date, or whether or not you will follow

the crowd. These choices have bigger consequences, and they usually take more time to make. The choice you make in some of these situations will greatly determine your future and life.

What about some of the choices you have made spiritually? We've talked about several of them over the last few weeks, and today we get to one of the biggest of all. This whole week we have been digging into the proof of spiritual growth that drives you to stop settling for less than all God has for you. Today we get to the key—check out what John 10:10 says about the kind of life that God has for you. This is one of the best *even mores* in this whole book—life more abundant. That's why Jesus came and died—so that you can have a more abundant life. How cool is that?

If a more abundant life is readily available through a relationship with Jesus Christ, then why don't more people choose that life? The answer is found at the beginning of today's passage. Our Enemy, the thief, is coming to steal, kill, and destroy our abundant lives. And guess what? He wants to steal our identities in Christ, kill our faith in the goodness of God, and destroy our hope. BUT you don't have to settle for that! Jesus came and died so that the Enemy wouldn't win. Don't allow Satan to keep you trapped in a lesser place. Live the abundant life in Christ.

When you really understand that *you* decide whether or not to live a more abundant life in Christ, you beat the Enemy at his own game. When you choose the abundant life and begin to grow in your relationship with Jesus, you become more and more empowered to live an *even more* abundant life in Him. Refuse to give the Enemy any ground in your life! That is the BEST choice you can make.

So, once you choose to have an abundant life in Christ, what choices do you need to make to continue growing in this relationship? And is it even worth it? Good questions. When it comes to furthering your relationship with the One who offers abundant life, remember what we talked about on Day 3 this week—pushing yourself. Choosing to live the abundant life will require us to go all-in and really focus on Jesus. When we're living for Him, we're living abundantly—in a bigger, better way than we ever thought possible! Let us focus on God and serving Him in every aspect of our lives, and we will see growth in our relationships with Him.

And for the record, the abundant life *is* worth it. When you go for the abundant life, you see yourself living full of the Holy Spirit and thus having the fruit of the Spirit flowing out of you. It is a life that has more impact—imagine more people being drawn to the way you reflect Jesus in different. Also, it is a life of joy and fulfillment. We were created to live in community with our Maker. When we choose the abundant life, we get a taste of how life is supposed to be—living with God and for God. We are all faced with the choice—choose abundance!

PRACTICE (JOURNAL & PRAY)

- In your journal, write down your answers to the following questions.
  - *Compare the two choices described today. Are you choosing a more abundant life or settling for less? Explain.*
  - *How would your life look different if you lived a more abundant life in Christ?*
- Spend some time in prayer. Ask for forgiveness for the times you've settled for less. Let God know that you want to live an abundant life in Him. Ask Him to help you see people and circumstances through His eyes so that you will not be tempted to settle.

LINGER

- Reread: John 10:10
- Dwell: Galatians 5:22-23
- Memorize: John 10:10

PROCEED

Use this section to keep moving forward as you apply the lesson to your daily life. Talk about it with someone you trust who can help you walk this spiritual journey with victory.

- Discuss the fruit of the Spirit found in Galatians 5:22-23. Which are most evident in your life? Which do you need the most right now? Why? When you look at the fruit from your life, does it show that you are living an abundant life in Christ? If not, what is it saying?
- Discuss specific things you can do to encourage one another in the challenge to live a life of abundance. Share where you struggle most with choosing abundance, then make a plan for what you will do to change that.

AUDACIOUS EXPECTATIONS

Now to him who is able to do immeasurably more than all we ask or imagine, according to his power that is at work within us, to him be glory in the church and in Christ Jesus throughout all generations, for ever and ever! Amen.

EPHESIANS 3:20-21

*W*hat kind of expectations do you have for your life? Have you even thought about it? Many of us simply function as if we're on auto-pilot until something happens that knocks us off course. However, we see all throughout Scripture that God has a plan and purpose for each of our lives—and that plan has been in place since before we were born (Jer. 1:5). I don't know about you, but I want to follow the Lord with my life and see what those plans are. God promises that His plans are even greater than anything we could dream!

The overarching theme throughout this book is *even more*, which was derived from Ephesians 3:20. This great verse is a conclusion to one of Paul's prayers for the church in Ephesus, and it is our prayer for you as well. Check out the full prayer below (vv. 14-21):

> For this reason I kneel before the Father from whom every family in heaven and on earth is named. I pray that He may grant you, according to the riches of His glory, to be strengthened with power in the inner man through His Spirit, and that the Messiah may dwell in your hearts through faith. I pray that you, being rooted and firmly established in love, may be able to comprehend with all the saints what is the length and width, height and depth of God's love, and to know the Messiah's love that surpasses knowledge, so you may be filled with all the fullness of God. Now to Him who is able to do above and beyond all that we ask or think according to the power that works in us—to Him be glory in the church and in Christ Jesus to all generations, forever and ever. Amen.
>
> **EPHESIANS 3:14-21**

Paul reminded us that God is ALMIGHTY GOD. He can do more than what we ask or even begin to understand. Paul wrote these words with such confidence and boldness, and my question for us today is this: *what if we lived with that same confidence in Almighty God, trusting that His goodness and love can overcome even our greatest shortcomings?*

To be able to live with such confidence, we must believe that He's able to do more "according to His power that is at work within us." Remember, this power refers to His Holy Spirit in our lives. May we recognize God for ALL He is able to do in and through us.

We only get one shot at this life. So, as we begin this last week, we want to challenge you to have audacious expectations for your life. You probably don't hear the word *audacious* on a daily basis, but it has become one of my favorite words to pray over my life. It means "very confident and daring; very bold and surprising or shocking." [5] In other words, we want you to have confident expectations that God will work through your life because you've given Him control.

Our hope is that the Lord would raise you up to live audaciously and have audacious expectations of God and His plans for your life. May you look forward to your future with great anticipation, expecting Him to use YOU to do great and mighty things for His kingdom. The Bible is full of stories of ordinary people who God used to do extraordinary things for Him. May you be one of those people!

Nothing is Impossible

But Jesus looked at them and said, "With men this is impossible, but with God all things are possible." Matthew 19:26

"Look, I am Yahweh, the God of all flesh. Is anything too difficult for Me?" Jeremiah 32:27

I love illusionists. In fact, I am their best audience member because I am fully entertained by it all. I love to have my mind blown by the crazy, unbelievable stunts they can pull. It's fascinating that they can do all the crazy things they do!

I have a friend who is one of the best illusionists in the country. He is a Christian, and he uses his talents for God's glory. He does some absolutely unbelievable tricks but he is always careful to point out that the tricks are actually just illusions—done by sleight of hand, distractions, etc. He also makes it very clear that his tricks pale in comparison to the amazing things that God can do.

It's really cool to think about how NOTHING is impossible with God. Our Lord doesn't need any tricks, sleight of hand, or distractions to accomplish big and powerful feats. Consider Matthew 19:26 and Jeremiah 32:27. Both of these verses state that nothing—absolutely nothing—is impossible for God. This is a truth that believers can stand on!

Maybe you struggle to fully understand that truth, and that's OK. It's a little hard to grasp that God can do literally anything that He pleases, especially since we as humans are so limited in our abilities. Even though you may struggle to completely process God's greatness, it is important to accept and believe its truth. Trusting that God can do absolutely anything will greatly shape the way you see Him. What problem is too big for God? None of them.

When the Bible says that nothing is impossible for God, it doesn't mean only a few things are impossible for God; it means *nothing* is impossible for Him. There are more verses that teach the truth of His greatness and power, and countless stories that prove He is indeed almighty. I mean, come on—the Red Sea parted, fire fell from heaven, a donkey talked out loud, a virgin gave birth, people were healed of leprosy, blind were given sight, the dead were raised, death was defeated—and those are just a few examples found in Scripture. Any one of these things is enough to blow your mind, because God's power is so much greater than even the most powerful people here on earth.

You may think that it would be easier to stand on the truth of God's power if you had seen any of these miracles take place. But consider the impossible things He has done in your life. He saved you from your sin. He speaks to you as a friend. He has directed you and protected you. Those are also miracles! Stand confident in the truth of His power because there is nothing that could happen in your life that He wouldn't be able to handle—nothing is impossible with God.

WORK IT OUT

PRACTICE (JOURNAL & PRAY)

- In your journal, write down your answers to the following questions.
  - *Do you really believe that God can do the impossible? Why or why not?*
  - *Do you think the way you live your life shows that you believe nothing is impossible with God? Explain.*
  - *What are some things you still need to trust God to handle?*
- Spend a few minutes in prayer, thanking God for specific evidences of His power in your life. Ask Him to increase your faith and grow it until it has no limits!

LINGER

- Reread: Jeremiah 32:27
- Dwell: Jeremiah 10:12
- Memorize: Matthew 19:26

PROCEED

Use this section to keep moving forward as you apply the lesson to your daily life. Talk about it with someone you trust who can help you walk this spiritual journey with victory.

- Read Jeremiah 10:12 out loud, and discuss how that verse affects your belief that God can do the impossible.
- Talk through different miracles from Scripture. Which one really blows your mind? How does it speak to God's greatness and power?
- Note that the God of the Bible is the same God we serve today. He is more than capable of blowing your mind with His greatness. What can you trust Him with today?
- Pray the words of Ephesians 1:15-29 over each other.

DAY 2

Miracles Still Happen

"I am the Alpha and the Omega—the beginning and the end,"
says the Lord God. "I am the one who is, who always was, and
who is still to come—the Almighty One." Revelation 1:8 (NLT)

Think back to some of your earliest memories of hearing stories from the Bible. You may have heard them from your parents, grandparents, Vacation Bible School, or Sunday school. What were your favorite stories? If you're anything like me, you may have been particularly drawn to the miracle stories because, well, those are awesome. Today, let's reflect on some of those stories.

The first miracle we find in Scripture is creation (Gen. 1–2). God created humanity, the earth, and everything in it. Then, in Genesis 6-9, we find the story of Noah. God used Noah to build an ark when the earth was flooded.

Moving on to the Book of Exodus, we see that God revealed Himself to Moses through a burning bush, then He performed all kinds of signs, miracles, and plagues to convince Pharaoh to let His people go. God also parted the Red Sea to allow the Israelites to escape the bondage of slavery in Egypt. And once they escaped, He provided manna and quail for them to eat—and it literally fell from heaven every day.

When the Israelites finally reached the promised land, God continued to do the miraculous. He parted the Jordan River and the Israelites crossed on dry ground. They defeated Jericho in an unprecedented marching attack. (Who ever said that band is not a real sport?)

Ladies, these are just a few of the miracles found in the pages of Scripture. There is story after story to remind us of God's power, character, ability, promises, and miracles. We can have confidence in Him because we have proof of His power through the stories in Scripture.

This God who impresses us with His power and creativity is the same God who has loved, forgiven, and redeemed us for His plan and His purposes. This is the God who says, "'I am the Alpha and the Omega,'" and "the One who is, who was, and who is coming, the Almighty" (Rev. 1:8). This is our God and He is still in the miracle-working business today! He is the same yesterday, today, and forever (Heb. 13:8).

Today is simply a time to remind you about your God. You serve a God who is all-powerful, all-knowing, compassionate, authoritative, patient, good and true! You can trust Him completely with your life and future. We pray you continue the challenge to stay in the Word and allow it to transform your heart, soul, and mind. Don't just skim through the Bible, but really dig into it and get to know your heavenly Father more intimately. If the stories of God's miracles don't fire you up, I'm not sure anything else will!

PRACTICE (JOURNAL & PRAY)

- In your journal, write down your answers to the following questions.
- *How does reading of God's works through Scripture grow in you a greater confidence in Him?*
- *Make a list of miracles you've personally witnessed or been a part of. How does seeing miracles affect your faith?*
- Pray for God to use you like he did the men and women from His Word. Thank Him for being the almighty God!

LINGER

- Reread: Revelation 1:8
- Dwell: John 3:16
- Memorize: Revelation 1:8

PROCEED

Use this section to keep moving forward as you apply the lesson to your daily life. Talk about it with someone you trust who can help you walk this spiritual journey with victory.

- Discuss some of the miracles mentioned today and talk about how God showed His greatness and faithfulness through those situations.
- Take some time to pray together. Ask God to enlarge your expectations of Him. Offer yourself as a vessel for Him to use however He sees fit.

DAY 3

You Don't Deserve It

Yahweh your God is among you, a warrior who saves. He will rejoice over you with gladness. He will bring you quietness with His love. He will delight in you with shouts of joy. Zephaniah 3:17

Therefore, since we have a great high priest who has passed through the heavens—Jesus the Son of God—let us hold fast to the confession. For we do not have a high priest who is unable to sympathize with our weaknesses, but One who has been tested in every way as we are, yet without sin. Therefore let us approach the throne of grace with boldness, so that we may receive mercy and find grace to help us at the proper time. Hebrews 4:14-16

Remember that time that you didn't study at all for a big test and ended up with an A? You didn't deserve it, but I know you appreciated it! Or maybe you received a gift that was out-of-this-world fantastic—like a car, outfit, or guitar. You didn't do anything to deserve the gift, but because of your relationship with the giver, the item is now yours.

The way you respond to those gifts says a lot about who you are. Too many people mistakenly believe that getting good things is simply what they are due—that somehow they deserve to receive awesome things. But if you recognize that the gift wasn't given because of what

you did, receiving something great will make you more humble. It makes me wonder—how do you and I respond to the wonderful, lavish gifts that the Lord gives us? Do we chalk them up as something we have earned or that we deserve?

Hopefully, you don't feel entitled to the Lord's gifts. The Bible is very clear that we are not deserving in any way of the glorious gifts God has chosen to bestow on us (and I can look at myself to see this truth). Yet, we continually receive them.

Now, you may be wondering what gifts we are talking about. Good question. Consider the gift of eternal life. In Romans 6:23 we read that "the wages of sin is death," and yet when we trust in Jesus, we get life instead of death. He gives us the gift of eternal life and forgiveness! That is lavish love at its best and we definitely don't deserve it. We also receive other gifts as His children, such as protection, grace, and community, to name a few. We don't deserve these good things, but God gives them to us because He loves and cares for us.

It just comes down to the character of God. Our God loves us with a lavish, unconditional, glorious, audacious love. We did nothing to earn it, but were created out of this very love. Look at how Zephaniah 3:17 describes the way God feels about you: "Yahweh your God is among you, a warrior who saves. He will rejoice over you with gladness. He will bring you quietness with His love. He will delight in you with shouts of joy." God not only saves you; He delights in you with "shouts of joy." Some versions translate the original language to say that He rejoices over you with singing. I love that picture! Those are strong feelings. In case you haven't noticed, you are really special to God. ALL of the good things that God has done and is going to do in your life are NOT about you; they are about Him. You don't deserve it, but He chooses to give you the abundant, glorious life just because He loves you. That's cool.

Here's some more good news. If you didn't do anything to deserve His love, then you can't do anything to have it taken away. Did you catch that? Since God loves you based on His lavish love for you and not what you've done, then there isn't anything you can do to change His feelings—they aren't conditional. That's a very freeing concept and should motivate you to continue raising your expectations of what God can do in your life! Fully receive His lavish love today.

WORK IT OUT

PRACTICE (JOURNAL & PRAY)

◆ In your journal, write down your answers to the following questions.
  ◆ *What are some of the greatest things that have happened to you lately? Did you deserve them? Explain.*
  ◆ *How do you feel about having good things happen even though you don't deserve them?*
  ◆ *Have you ever struggled to accept God's lavish love for you? Why or why not?*
  ◆ *The Bible says that every perfect gift is from above (Jas. 1:17). What do you need to thank God for today?*
◆ Write out James 1:17 on a note card and keep it in a place where you will see it often (maybe as a bookmark in your Bible or as a screen saver on your phone). When you see that verse, use it as a reminder to worship and thank God for His good gifts to you.

LINGER

◆ Reread: Hebrews 4:14-16
◆ Dwell: James 1:17
◆ Memorize: Zephaniah 3:17

PROCEED

Use this section to keep moving forward as you apply the lesson to your daily life. Talk about it with someone you trust who can help you walk this spiritual journey with victory.

◆ Talk about how you feel when you realize that you don't deserve the good things you receive.
◆ Describe how it feels to know God rejoices over you.
◆ Discuss some ways to respond to the Lord's love for you.

DAY 4

Dream Big!

Don't copy the behavior and customs of this world, but let God transform you into a new person by changing the way you think. Then you will learn to know God's will for you, which is good and pleasing and perfect. Romans 12:2 (NLT)

Take a moment to look back at the journey you've been on these past few weeks. It's a healthy thing to reflect on what you've learned about yourself and the Lord. At some point the past few weeks, you may have had to face some hard truths, but working through that sin or struggle will help you live an *even more* life in Christ.

Those negative things that you've been through do not have to define you or affect who you are in your relationship with the Lord. Remember Jeremiah 29:11: "'For I know the plans I have for you'—this is the LORD's declaration—'plans for your welfare, not for disaster, to give you a future and a hope.'" Jesus knows the plans that He has for your life. You aren't what you've done, who you were, or where you've been. You are His child, bought at a price and dearly loved. God will work in and through your life if you allow Him to, regardless of your past. You have an opportunity to play a part of God's bigger story.

Not only is it healthy to recognize what Jesus has brought us through, but it is also important to look forward with vision and

dream with our God. We pray that you begin to pray for a bigger vision for your life. Ask for a God-sized vision, and dream with Him about things you can do for His glory! May you not remain focused on your past, but dream BIG dreams with God about what your place is in His story.

What is God's bigger story for you? Have you ever stopped to think about how exciting your life could be if you decided to pray with expectation about what God could do through your life? Remember the introduction to this week—God can do infinitely, abundantly MORE than anything that we could ask or imagine (Eph.3:20). So why not dream big? Why not live in a way that is bold and passionate about following God? Any time we make a decision to move forward and "go with God," we can always expect opposition from our Enemy. But remember: "the One who is in you is greater than the one who is in the world" (1 John 4:4).

You may be thinking, *I want to dream big, but I know how small and limited I am.* While it's possible to overestimate our own abilities, we can never overestimate what God can do. When we pray with boldness and dream with expectation, God will refine us, making us into the women that He wants us to become. He will transform us through the way we think, our focus, and our actions. God will work in and through us to glorify Himself. And that's really the key—God should be glorified through our big dreams, not ourselves. I know we've discussed the importance of our lives bringing Him glory a lot these past eight weeks, but we can't drive home that point enough. This life is not about us. What an honor it is that He allows us to be a part of His story. We need to consciously lay down our plans for personal gain at His feet and allow God to work through us in the way He sees best.

Girls, always go with God. Dream God-honoring dreams and pray and seek the Lord as you hold on for an amazing adventure with your heavenly Father.

PRACTICE (JOURNAL & PRAY)

◆ In your journal, write down your answers to the following questions.

- ◆ *What do you want to see God do in your life?*
- ◆ *How do you think God can use the gifts and talents He has given you to bring Him glory?*

◆ Take some time to pray and journal over dreams for your life. Praise God for His good gifts, especially the gift of salvation. Thank Him for all He has done for you and what He is going to do through your life.

LINGER

Reread: Romans 12:2
Dwell: Jeremiah 29:11; 1 John 4:4
Memorize: John 10:10b

PROCEED

Use this section to keep moving forward as you apply the lesson to your daily life. Talk about it with someone you trust who can help you walk this spiritual journey with victory.

◆ As you begin to wrap up this study, revisit some of the questions in the "Practice" sections thus far. Share praises about where He has brought you from and dream together about what He wants to do in and through your lives in the future!

DAY 5 *Gloriously Rich*

His divine power has given us everything required for life and godliness through the knowledge of Him who called us by His own glory and goodness. By these He has given us very great and precious promises, so that through them you may share in the divine nature, escaping the corruption that is in the world because of evil desires. 2 Peter 1:3-4

Oh my! You have made it through this 40-day journey in pursuing an *even more* life in Christ! That's incredible, and we hope that you are blown away with the growth you are seeing in your relationship with God. You have now studied eight different proofs of your faith, and our prayer is that God has begun to transform your heart throughout this journey with Him. Before we turn the last page of this experience, let's talk about one more factor to consider as you develop your audacious expectations.

Let's begin with this question: *who are the richest people you know?* Most of us think of famous entertainers, actors, or athletes when we think of individuals with lots of money. How would you respond to the person who called you rich? You would probably point out that compared to other people, you aren't wealthy at all. But compared to people in third world countries, you are beyond wealthy.

In reality, you really are gloriously rich no matter how much money you have. You're probably wondering how that can be true. Second Peter 1:3-4 offers some clarity. It says, "His divine power has given us

everything required for life and godliness through the knowledge of Him who called us by His own glory and goodness. By these He has given us very great and precious promises ..." What all have you been given according to these verses? EVERYTHING. We have been given everything we need for life and godliness. That is a great promise from God. That, my friends, means that you are gloriously rich, and you should start living like it.

Have you ever noticed how wealthy people act differently? They make decisions differently. Why? Because they know that their wealth will back them up. Their monetary possessions will open doors and allow them opportunities—almost as if they have the right to be certain places and act certain ways because of their money. Guess what? You are gloriously rich, and you have the right to live like a daughter of the KING of KINGS.

That wealth is way greater than the wealth of someone with a large bank account. What if you began living with great expectations, knowing that you posses a supernatural power through the Holy Spirit? This passage also points out that you've been given everything you need by His divine power. That's the best kind of power, and it's at work on your behalf all the time.

How is it that someone who has that kind of power and wealth can be bankrupt? You can be spiritually bankrupt when you are not listening to the truth of God's Word, but are instead listening to the lies of the Enemy. Don't let him keep you from living the victorious, powerful life that God has for you.

You've been given everything you need. His power is for you. You are gloriously rich.

It's definitely time you start living like it!

PRACTICE (JOURNAL & PRAY)

- In your journal, write down your answers to the following questions.
  - *Do you live like someone who is rich in Christ or spiritually bankrupt? Explain.*
  - *Where do you need to raise your expectations of what His power can do?*

LINGER

- Reread: 2 Peter 1:3-4
- Dwell: Ephesians 3:14-19
- Memorize: 2 Peter 1:3

PROCEED

Use this section to keep moving forward as you apply the lesson to your daily life. Talk about it with someone you trust who can help you walk this spiritual journey with victory.

- Discuss how the knowledge of God ties in with receiving what you need for life and godliness.
- Talk through different ways that you know Him better because of this experience over the last 40 days.
- Pray this prayer from Ephesians 3:14-19 for each other. (Consider getting on your knees as you pray):
  - *"For this reason I kneel before the Father from whom every family in heaven and on earth is named. I pray that He may grant you, according to the riches of His glory, to be strengthened with power in the inner man through His Spirit, and that the Messiah may dwell in your hearts through faith. I pray that you, being rooted and firmly established in love, may be able to comprehend with all the saints what is the length and width, height and depth of God's love, and to know the Messiah's love that surpasses knowledge, so you may be filled with all the fullness of God."*

Wrap Up

♦ How have you been challenged to live an even more life in Christ over the past 40 days?

♦ What areas of your life need to experience transformation most? Are you willing to surrender these areas of your life to Christ? Why or why not?

♦ How has this study shaped your expectations of the work Christ can and will do through you?

♦ How does your life show "proof" of the relationship you have with God? How can others benefit from seeing these proofs in your life?

God created you to have an abundant life in Him, but you must make the daily choice to live for Him, following His plan for your life, not your own. Though you will face struggles and roadblocks along the way, God will be faithful to grow you into the woman that He wants you to be as you press forward and pursue an *even more* life in Him. As you allow Christ to transform your heart, soul, and mind, others will see Jesus through the life change taking place.

DISCUSSION GUIDE

Tips for Small Groups

We are thrilled that you have chosen to walk through this 40 day journey with a small group! Significant life-change can take place within a small group of trusted peers and friends or with a mentor. God created us with an inner desire to belong in community. This resource provides you a discussion guide over the next eight weeks that will be both challenging and rewarding for you and the group you're leading.

We want you to feel confident and prepared to lead your group each week. Use the Discussion Guide to help you navigate the weekly studies. Also, check out the following Bible study tools to enhance your discussion:

- *Bible Commentary*—Detailed theological analysis of specific verses and passages of Scripture. Includes a background introductory section for each book of the Bible, followed by detailed commentary of Scripture verse by verse.

- *Bible Concordance*—Alphabetical index of important words in Scripture and the references of texts in which they are found.

- *Bible Encyclopedia*—Articles about Bible characters, events, and places, including history, religious environment, culture, language, and literature, as well as cross-references to related Scripture verses.

- *Topical Bible*—Bible references to topics addressed or mentioned in the Bible.

- *Online Resources*—The website *www.mystudybible.com* offers free online tools for reading and studying the Bible.[6]

INTRO SESSION

As your group meets weekly to discuss and review the material covered in each proof, use the suggested guide provided in this section for additional illustrations and creative elements.

Bring in a dying, wilted plant and a beautiful, healthy plant. If this is not possible, print off pictures of both dying and healthy plants, and post them on the walls around the room. When members of the group enter the room, ask them to pick which plant or picture they like best. Most likely, they will be drawn to the thriving, healthy plant.

Talk about how plants without deep roots in good soil stand no chance of surviving. Point out that no amount of water, sunlight, or care can revive a plant that has poor or shallow roots. It simply won't grow correctly.

Guide group to understand that as believers, our roots are based in our relationship with Jesus Christ. But if our roots are not deep and secure, the trials or life, our struggles with sin, and convincing lies from the Enemy may keep us from fully following God and becoming the women that He wants us to be.

Share that through this study we will learn how to have an *even more* life in Christ. Each week we will discuss a different "proof" that Christ is working in and through us—through our desires, relationships, words, and deeds. We will focus on some ways you may have already been experiencing change as well as talk about what to do if the change hasn't been happening.

Hand out books and go over the "How to Use" section (p.11). Discuss the daily "Work It Out" section and how each person should dive in and fully utilize that section during their alone time in the Word.

Inform the group that they are going to be "food critics" for the night. Bring in a few samples, both of foods that you know they will love (ex: chocolate) and foods that they may be opposed to (ex: blue cheese). Prior to handing out samples, pass out small slips of paper and a pen to each group member. Guide them to then rank the samples from favorite to least favorite taste. After all the foods have been sampled, tally the results and declare which food was the most popular.

Discuss which foods they were most drawn to and why.

Point out that we all have different food cravings. Discuss other things we crave in life, like a good night's sleep or summer break. Then ask the following question: Do you crave Jesus in your life?

Talk about how our "cravings" begin to change as we grow in our walks with Christ. We will become motivated by different desires and tastes, and our focus will shift from the things of this world to the things of God.

Discuss the Proceed section from each day of this week. Discuss their answers to some of the questions in that section. Help them process through ways they've seen their tastes change since following Christ. (Guide them to come up with specific changes they have noticed in regards to their focus, appearance, words, deeds, relationships, etc.)

Print off some images of famous labels (i.e. the Nike© swoosh™, the Starbucks© lady, etc.). Point out some of the labels, and lead the group to identify what brand the symbol represents. Most likely, they will have no trouble identifying the brands, because the symbols are so common in our culture.

After showing the famous labels, show a picture of a cross. Ask: What does this symbol represent?

Allow the group to discuss that a cross represents Jesus' death, burial, and resurrection. It's most often a symbol of Christianity. Point out that many people wear cross necklaces, display crosses in their homes, or even hang small crosses from their rear view mirrors. Ask: Just because someone wears a cross necklace or decorates with crosses, does that make them a Christian? Explain.

Point out that simply wearing a cross—or even going to church or claiming the label "Christian"—doesn't actually make you someone who follows Christ. Being a Christian is not about simply attaching a label to your life; it is about conforming to the image of Christ through every facet of your life.

Help your group understand that as Christians, we are to be unique in the way we act, talk, and through our influence. Discuss some of the their answers to the questions posed in the Proceed sections throughout this week.

Guide the group to come up with a sales pitch for an item of your choice. Make sure that the item they are "selling" is really ridiculous, like a leash for a pet hamster or a brocolli-flavored candy bar. If they push back on the ridiculous item, that's OK; the goal is for them to struggle to convincingly "sell" their products.

Allow a few minutes for the group to come up with their sales pitch, and then guide them to try "selling" you on the product.

Discuss the activity. Ask: Was it hard to "sell" something you thought was ridiculous? Do you think you convinced me to buy that product?

Point out that we must believe in something to convincingly sell it to someone else. In the same way, we must be confident in our belief in God to influence others for Christ.

Say: This week walks through some of the basics of the faith so that you can learn to reinforce your own beliefs. Confidence in your faith will help you stand firm against opposition and will draw others to know Christ as Lord.

Talk through some of the their answers to the Proceed section questions. Pray that they may have a confident faith in the truth of God and His Word.

Discuss the idea of "frenemies," as described in the introduction to week four. Refer to the movie *Mean Girls* (Paramount, 2004) or another film that depicts someone who appears to be a friend, but is actually an enemy. Guide your group to understand that the term "frenemy" is a huge contradiction. You can't be a friend while also being an enemy.

Discuss our real enemy, Satan. Ask: Do you think Satan plays an active role in our world? In your life?

Read John 10:10 aloud. Explain that the Enemy does not want our good, but remind your group that as believers they have God's Holy Spirit at work in their lives to help them when tempted by Satan's lies.

Briefly discuss days 1 and 2. Bring clarity to any confusion on what spiritual warfare is and what it is not.

Help them understand that God has equipped us to stand strong against our Enemy. Remind them that God's Word, the Bible, is our best defense against Satan's attacks.

Spend some time praying over each group member, that she may stand strong against the Enemy and live a life that honors God.

Inform your group that they are going to play "Rock, Paper, Scissors." Lead them to pair up and play their first round. Once winners are declared, guide them to pair up and play again. Continue to play until two members remain. Then allow them to play a final match and declare a winner. Consider bringing a small prize for the winner, such as a treat or $5 gift card.

Debrief the game. Discuss the competitive nature of a game, even one you have no control over, such as "Rock, Paper, Scissors." Ask: Why is victory so important to people?

Point out that victory is indeed a big goal for most people in school, sports, relationships, etc., but our primary focus as believers should be victory in our spiritual lives.

Discuss the questions posed in the introduction for Proof #5.
- *What are some things that you do and say that leans more toward spiritual defeat than spiritual victory?*
- *What areas of your life are you making choices that don't set you up for a win?*
- *Does your attitude tell people that you are planning to settle for loss when you could be reaching for victory? Explain.*

Remind your group that we have a real Enemy who wants to "steal and to kill and to destroy" (John 10:10). He desires to keep us from victory in Christ, but then, talk through some of the ways they can live in spiritual victory, not defeat.

Spend a few minutes discussing answers to some of the Proceed questions.

If appropriate for the age of the members in your group, bring in some information on current human trafficking statistics. Point out that these people are literally trapped in their slavery.

As an added activity, spend the first or last few minutes of your group meeting in a prayer time for those enslaved in human trafficking throughout the world.

Say: It sounds horrible to be enslaved, but that's how we often live our lives—enslaved to sin.

Point out that God desires for us to live in freedom. Some of us, though saved, still live as if we are slaves to sin.

Ask: In what areas of your life do you still live as a slave? Why?

Emphasize that only when we find freedom in Christ can we help others find freedom as well.

Be sensitive when approaching this topic. Some group members may feel uncomfortable being open and honest about their struggles with sin. Remind them that you are always available to talk, even outside of the group meeting time.

Discuss some of the answers to the Practice section questions.

Pray that each person might experience true freedom in Christ—the freedom that the heavenly Father desires for believers to live in.

Discuss the idea of "settling." Point out that, in general, "settling" has a negative connotation. As an example, bring up times when families are trying to choose a place to eat. Maybe a few potential restaurants are mentioned, and likely, everyone has a different opinion on what sounds good. Typically after some debate, the family settles on a place. When you settle, you're usually compromising or giving in. It may not be your first choice, but you're hungry, so you settle.

Point out that we often settle for a defeated life instead of a life of victory in Christ. Ask: Why do you think we settle for defeat?

Ask: What does it mean to you to live abundantly in Christ? Why might that seem like a hard thing to do?

Call on a group member to read 1 Timothy 4:7-8 aloud, and discuss how we can "train ourselves in godliness." Then, connect the concepts of abundant life and godliness. Ask: How are the two things related? Can you experience an abundant life in Christ without pursuing godliness? Explain.

Discuss the "training plans," as mentioned in the Proceed section of day 3. Encourage group members to share their ideas for training in godliness, and hold them accountable to keep up with their plans.

Reinforce the idea that we should not settle for living in defeat, but rather should strive for victory in Christ. Achieving victory will take effort, but it is worth it in the long run to live the abundant life that God wants for us.

Pass out a sheet of paper and a pen to every person in the room. Direct them to list five expectations they have for their lives on the sheets of paper. For example, one expectation might be to graduate college one day; another might be to buy a house as some point in their lives. After they've had some time to compile a list, allow them to share a few of their expectations with the class.

Then, lead them to make a second list on the back side of their paper with expectations they have of God. This may be a harder task. After a few minutes, allow them to share their lists.

Say: We can easily come up with expectations for our own lives—goals we want to accomplish and things we want to do. But those expectations are typically focused on ourselves. This week, we learned that we should have audacious expectations—both for ourselves and for God. But these expectations should focus on ways that God can use us to bring Him glory, rather than ways that we can bring ourselves glory. When you give Him control of your life, you can be confident that He will work in you and through you.

Ask: Does your life show that you believe nothing is impossible with God? Explain.

Discuss some of the group's answers to the questions in the Practice section. Clarify any confusion they may have, and pray that they would have audacious expectations of God because He is at work in their lives.

JOURNAL

JOURNAL

JOURNAL

JOURNAL

JOURNAL

JOURNAL

JOURNAL

JOURNAL

SOURCES

1. "Influence," *Merriam-Webster* [online], [accessed 11 June 2015]. Available from the Internet: *www.merriam-webster.com/dictionary/influence*

2. James Strong, *Strong's Complete Word Study Concordance*, (Chattanooga, TN: 2004).

3. Euan McKirdy, "World has 35.8 million slaves, report finds," *CNN* [online], 4 January 2015 [accessed 11 June 2015]. Available from the Internet: *www.cnn.com/2014/11/17/world/walk-free-global-slavery-index-2014/*

4. *Holman Bible Dictionary*, (Nashville, TN: Holman Bible Publishers).

5. "Audacious," *Merriam-Webster* [online], [accessed 11 June 2015]. Available from the Internet: *www.merriam-webster.com/dictionary/audacious*

6. Adapted from *Read the Bible for Life* Leader Kit. Item 005253507. Published by LifeWay Press®. © 2010
George H. Guthrie. Made in the USA. Reproduction rights granted.

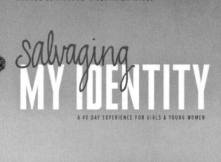